The Cathedral

THE
CATHEDRAL

Clive Sansom

METHUEN & CO LTD
36 ESSEX STREET · LONDON W.C.2

W5010
200 29566

Catalogue No 5998/U

Printed in Great Britain
by The Camelot Press Ltd, Southampton

While they lasted . . . they were not the Middle Ages at all. They hadn't the faintest idea that they were medieval.

JOHN LIVINGSTON LOWES

Contents

Spirit of the Cathedral

WHATEVER is beautiful, whatever rouses
  The heart from its complacent sleep, says
'Man, you are more than man, more
Than a repository of birth and death'—such beauty,
Before the creative chisel of the mind
Shaped it in stone or word, music
Or colour, lay in the Imagination's eye,
The retina of God.

They know, who see it, that a world exists
Behind the world, where the thought, the Idea
Of beauty, independent of its earthly form,
Lives in perfection—an eternal realm
Which holds the immaculate pattern fast
The artist gropes to find. But being
Artist he must grope, must mould
Within his mouldering hands a symbol
Of that perfection—loveliness dissolving
Even as it leaves his touch, but telling
For a space of time, of beauty free
Of space and time. And beholders know
The shadow's substance, the divine matrix
From which this image came.

So with the Cathedral. Before it laid
Its pressure on the clay, enclosed the moving
Air with arches, or threw its spire
Upon the mercy of the wind—already in that other
Kingdom stood the great archetype,
Supreme and perfect, waiting only
The man to see, the will to fashion
Its mortal replica.

11

The Land

Like the palm of an open hand
These meadows lie.
Like fingers slightly raised
To the circling sky

Five valleys meet,
And slide their streams
Into this limpid place
Timeless as dreams;

Mingle their music with the birds'
And then, as one,
Find their eternal way
To the sea and sun.

Invaders, wave on wave,
Have crossed this land—
Columned ants on the skin
Of a stretched hand.

Iberian, Celt, Roman,
Teuton and Dane
Have poured from the sea northward
To the Great Plain;

Have ringed their temples there,
Balanced them high
Against the unrolling god-land
Of cloud and sky;
Built dyke and rampart,
Fought and fled,
Dug their long barrows there,
Buried their dead;

Or, sheeping those chalk downs
In upland air,
Have shorn them clean of scrub,
Curving and bare.

But here, where river met
Forest and fen,
They left the land untouched,
Unhoused by men

Till Saxons felled the woods,
Drained marsh away,
And in water-meadows of smooth green
Their cattle lay.

Now Normans claim this place
Of grass and reeds
As glebe and manor-lands
For their bishop's needs,

Taking butter and brawn
For his Plain-bound priests,
Fish for their Friday fast,
Duck for their feasts. . . .

For a while the land rests.
Freed from the weight
Of woods, it stretches in the sun
And breathes the late

Warm air of Spring.
All that the past creates
Is now forgotten; and the land,
The land waits.

Peasant's Daughter

THIRTEENTH CENTURY

AMONG meads many my mother bore me,
    Where brooks meandering met under boughs.
Ewe-leaze and kine-yard were all my dwelling,
Hurdles that sheltered the shorn lamb.
At Thane's bidding, they being his bondsmen,
My father's kin felled fierce the woods,
Down to their knees brought many a beech-lord,
With heavy billhook hewed their limbs.
Then, in its stead, this farmland fashioning,
Meat they brought to their master's board.
Such the country in childhood I cherished,
Where crinkled cowslip and gildcup grew.
Lying in grass, as to lark I listened,
Sky was a wonder of cloud and song.

Then, on a season, my seventh summer,
Came dire tidings, deeds most dreadful—
All these leasings, long held by labour,
Lush meadlands set between streams,
For a towered church, for tombs taken!
At bailiff's word were we sent southward
To land in sad heart, half won from wildness,
Where all folk, churls and churls' children,
With toil yearlong and many a hard task,
Must forage food for the Bishop's builders.
Seldom I walk where in youth I wandered,
Where brooks meandering met in meads.
At every step I see lost lark's-nest,
Trampled cowslips, the covered sky.

Bishop

THIRTEENTH CENTURY

BISHOP:

I RICHARD LE JEUN, Bishop, being
, In my sixty-third year translated to the see of York
Do make these records of my undertakings. . . .

Our lot was hard, living in the King's land
High on the Great Plain with winds for company,
Imprisoned there in the midst of a vast fortress,
Earth-ramparts surrounding us, and a towering keep
Dwarfing the Church of God. Nor was that all:
The garrison, leaders and led alike,
Being the King's men, openly slighted us,
Seeking our humiliation on all occasions.
For more than a hundred years we endured these things,
Praying a saint's patience. But some demurred:

PETER OF BLOIS:

Brothers! it is not 'patience' to endure hurts
Which our decision and labour can swiftly amend.
Why suffer wind and cold, and bowmen's mockery,
When in a few years, by our own efforts,
We can remove ourselves from the barbs of both?
What does the Church of God with the castles of men?
Shall the Ark of the Covenant be held forever
In the Temple of Baal? Nay, in God's name,
Let us descend from the Plain. Below is Canaan—
There lie meadows and fertile valleys abounding
In the fruits of the earth, watered by living streams.
There is such a site for God's church
As in the whole world finds no parallel!

BISHOP:

My brother, Herbert le Jeun, then Bishop,
Took no action, until at Rogationtide
In the year of his death—twelve hundred and seventeen
In Our Lord's reckoning—we made our procession
Through the Church's land, visiting farms
And manors, chanting litanies as is is our custom.
These performed, returning to the castle at nightfall
And finding all gates barred against us,
We slept in ditches in the shelter of a stockade
With soldiers' laughter echoing from the walls above,
And a vile tempest howling in our ears.
They called us drunkenly: 'Sons of a bishop's concubine!'—
A statement which, though true and known to many,
Lacked the dignity of ecclesiastical etiquette,
Nor was conducive to good discipline.
Next morning, in full Chapter, above coughs and sneezes,
My brother voiced our final resolution:—

HERBERT LE JEUN:

I will labour earnestly to build an abode and church
Far from this fortress and removed from the King's power.

BISHOP:

We therefore, between us, framing a petition,
Despatched it to Pope Honorius by special messenger:—

MESSENGER:

Holiness: thy servants under God,
We beg thy intercession on behalf of our labours.
This Church, a prisoner within a fortress,
Is subject to such discomfort and oppression
We reside here longer at peril to our lives.
Our house is rocked by collision of the wind, and the abuse
Of soldiery. Our roof is broken. The sound of wind
Drowns voices of our priests at their high offices;

The cold of the wind brings winter suffering.
Our only water, (save that through the roof itself),
Is brought from afar at extortionate prices.
We may not enter or leave the precincts of this building
Without permission from the Castellan. On Holy Thursday,
On Ash Wednesday when the Lord's Supper is administered,
At the time of Synod or the ordination of clerks,
The faithful who would visit us from beyond the city
Are denied access on the grounds of military security.
We pray thee, therefore, as our Father in God,
Grant us permission to abandon this hill-prison
And build again beyond its jurisdiction.

BISHOP:

Even as the messenger bore these words, my brother
Died; and I, elected in his stead,
Received the papal Nuncio and confirmed their truth.
Within a year from Rome these tidings:

POPE HONORIUS:

Honorius, Bishop, Servant of the Servants of God,
To our reverend bishop, Richard, brother in Christ,
And to our beloved sons, the Dean and Chapter, greetings!
We gave our mandate to Guido, legate and cardinal,
Carefully to enquire into all things concerning you,
And faithfully to report to us the result of his findings.
These depositions, sealed under his seal,
Being diligently examined by our chaplain,
We find these complaints most adequately proved,
And do, on our authority by God conferred,
Grant you free power to transfer your church
To a worthier site within that diocese.
And be it known further that whoever in any sort
Shall seek to infringe the tenor of this grant,
Or to presume rashly to oppose the same,
Shall incur the indignation of Almighty God,

And of Peter, blessèd saint, his apostle,
To whose glory and honour this Cathedral is dedicate.
Dated this fourth day of the Calends of April,
In the second year of our Pontificate. . . .

BISHOP:

On receiving these words, I informed the Chapter,
Went to the altar, knelt, and praised God.
Then alone, with none attending, I walked down—
Down from the bleak, unlovely Plain, to the meadows
That were green with willow, golden with buttercups.
In the Boundary Fields, at the angle of three rivers,
I sat down. I sat in the long grass
And, for the first time in many years,
Sat without thought, without prayer,
Feeling only the sun and the soft wind.
And as I dreamed, a vision. . . . I saw
From the fields before me the great walls rise
That would be a monument for ever to the Glory of God,
The love and labour of man. I saw it grow
Like living trees—stiff buttresses spreading
With arches, with branched gables and lancets;
The West Front clustered as thick with saints
As berries on a holly-bush; and high above,
In his niche under the topmost architrave, the blessèd Peter,
Raising his hand in joyful benediction.

Quarry-Master

THIRTEENTH CENTURY

HERE is its birthplace; this vast cave
The womb of our Cathedral, where we, her quarrymen,
Laboured to ease her labour,
Delivering it stone by stone. From here
We sent each block by handcart and bullock-wagon,

Or floated it by stream to Dorbury Meadows
To be hewn and carved from neutral freestone
Into arch and column, niche and capital,
Until it rose complete—a single building
Formed from ten thousand parts.

But here the rock still holds
The shape of a cathedral, as grasses bear
The seal of the risen deer. Look there,
Now I have lit the torch! See
That tremendous nave, its double aisles—
Two lines of columns, pillars
Of unhewn stone—left standing
Eighty, ninety feet, to hold
The hidden roof—advancing and receding
At the torch's whim.

                        Sometimes,
Standing here, I fancy this
Has the greater beauty, this mother church
Crude and half-created, yet capable
Of incredible births, like Lilith,
Mother of Eve. . . . Who knows
What wonder or monster may crawl from here
Where Time's torch cannot reach?

Dedication

THIRTEENTH CENTURY

OF course I remember.—April, the Feast of Vitalis,
The year my first was born. A time of showers,
And priests from all over the three counties.

19

What did they do, those priests? What else
But take off their shoes, every shaved man of them,
And paddle in the wet grass! Then they sang.
They sang the Litany of the Saints in the soft rain,
With drops runneling their cheeks, mixing with their singing,
And crawling wantonly down the lips of their saltires.
The King there? No, he would have been,
But he was away on the border, fighting the Welsh—
Or making a treaty with them, the same thing.
So were the nobles—except for our own Earl.
He and his wife were there. Poor man!
He little thought he'd be dead within five years
And buried in that very cathedral—the first to be put there,
And a lovely tomb. . . . Now what was I saying?
Yes, it left off raining as they stopped singing,
And the birds took up—you know how they do
After a Spring shower—so it was hard to follow
The Bishop's sermon. But that didn't matter:
We saw him laying the first three stones.
One for the Pope, they said, another for the Archbishop,
And a third for himself. *And* he deserved it,
Him having the trouble of it all and the wet feet.
Well then, Longespée, he laid a stone;
Then his lady; then the dean and chanter,
The chancellor, treasurer, archdeacons and canons—
A stone apiece so nobody would be left out—
Some rolling up their sleeves and doing it properly,
Some fussing and fumbling with their little trowel
Till I wanted to snatch it from them and do it myself;
And all the time those birds singing and singing. . . .
Then they put on their shoes again and traipsed off.

Architect

THIRTEENTH CENTURY

I

Those men, our fathers, returning from the First Crusade,
 Brought more than defeat, more even than victory:
They brought from Jerusalem the pointed arch—though Euclid
Had found it first. No mere device or decoration,
But like the wheel and alphabet it opened a new world,
A new dimension. . . . It made possible
The groined vault with its leaping height, its weight
Not taken by the wall beneath the arch, but distributed
To piers and buttresses, leaving the wall itself
A thin shell, broken by many windows—
Every stone given its work to do,
Construction everywhere exposed, like the actions and motives
Of men who are unshamed and unafraid.
For that's the delight of the new architecture:
One sees here, not the peace of inertia,
But the poise that comes from the balance of opposing forces,
As in the character of a great man—a calm
Active, not passive—dynamic certainty!
In a word, sir, since you are a poet
And have your critics too, the difference between metre—
The counting of syllables on placid fingers—and rhythm,
The very articulation of the senses. . . .
What's more, body and spirit being so entwined,
It speaks for our religion as the Roman never spoke.
Instead of the cautious calculation of the intellect,
Following a rule of thumb, the daring flight
Of the soul toward heaven—God's spirit in the stone.

II

Ah, what joy to be alive at such a season!
To be young—to flower when an idea is flowering!

Do you wonder I look back to happiness?
There I see them—Canterbury, Chichester, Lincoln—
In the springtime of their being, with the dew upon them.
Within fifty years a new style was perfected,
And I, Henry Falcon, for half that time
Apprentice, mason, travelling mason, and finally
Magister latomorum, master-mason,
Taking my eightpence a day, with food and fuel,
A cask of wine, forty-six holidays a year,
And a squire's robe, fur-trimmed, at Michaelmas.
Then here, at last, the greatest of opportunities—
Interviewed, questioned, cross-questioned, appointed—
Not the refashioning of an established church,
Raising walls, adding vault and clerestory,
But the erection of a complete cathedral on a site
New and untrammelled. . . . Look forward you may
To Paradise. Do you wonder that I look back?

III

But I'd not reckoned with Master Jocelyn of Derby,
Fabric Master, Clerk of Works, go-between
And general factotum, thrusting his quill
In my face at the least provocation. Believe me, sir,
No art ever came from a committee,
None. That's where you're fortunate in your profession,
Though it may be less profitable. No group of busybodies
Tosses the subject and its treatment at you, and dictates
The words into your poem. . . . But in building
There's not a minor canon or chapterhouse cleaner
Who can't instruct you in the moulding of a capital,
And knows more about vault-spanning than you know yourself.
This Jocelyn, too, had handled a chisel once
And chipped some tombs when the sacristan wasn't looking—
Durham, I believe, or Exeter. In the trade
He'd have been my block-boy at three ha'pence a day,
But put a cope on him and he's my equal!

22

He wanted the French design of Rouen
Or Amiens, transplanted holus bolus
And dumped on an English meadow. I lectured them
On the essential difference between the characters
Of French and English, what is right for one,
As I explained to them—ornate and decorative—
Being wrong for the other, with his queer streak of austerity,
Who always prefers the strong sweep of the whole
To elaboration of detail. I scored that point.
Then Master Jocelyn demanded that at least the sandstone
Should come from Northern France—because at Canterbury
It came from there. Again I harangued the Chapter:
'Why import it from Caen, at vast expense,
When stone as fine may be quarried at your own doorstep?'
'Besides,' I argued, 'drawing it from our English earth,
The Cathedral it becomes will be a natural outcrop,
Belonging to our soil as well as to our soul!'
The alliteration won them. Jocelyn concurred,
Without conviction. Nor did he forgive.

IV

Next he objected to my bay-design.
'These main arcades too low,' he told my drawings,
Poking them with his stick. (They lay, seven yards of vellum,
Rolled out on the Chapter-house floor). 'There!—
These arches should be raised. As for the triforium. . . .'
I spoke, but to no purpose. What did they care
For balance and proportion, the basic principles
Of building? All they knew: in three contests
I had scored twice. Now was Jocelyn's turn.
Next the spire. No spire, he said.
A low, dwarfed, dwindled tower like Westminster's
Was all that we required. As for expense
(Conveniently forgotten when advocate for French stone)
A spire was inexcusable extravagance.
With his Treasurer's help—for money, have you noticed,

Has a habit of expanding and contracting with the speaker's
                                                                mind—
A spire would lead them all (here he raised
One stiff admonitory prophet's finger)
To bankruptcy and perdition. . . . I hoped to trick them
By strengthening the foundations at the crossing, building pillars
To take a spire's weight if Master Jocelyn,
With my great good-will, should knock at Purgatory
Ahead of expectation. . . . But no,
He was too shrewd for me, like a schoolmaster
With nose for errors only. . . . Ah well,
He's gone now, God rest his soul.
(After a suitable period of expiation!)
No doubt, like spiders, snakes, pain and the plague,
He filled some purpose in a wider scheme. I wonder. . . .

v

At last, after long discussion, the ground-plan was approved.
We inked the drawings in. Then the night vigil
A week from the summer solstice—St Peter's Eve—
Waiting, with prayers and uneasy slumber, for dawn
To colour the long skyline on the eastward plain.
As the first rays broke, we set a rod
Exactly between the sun and altar-site, fixing
The line of orientation; and in that trance
Which follows a wakeful night, we marked the plan,
Cutting the outline of the drawings into the clean turf,
While the anthem of First Vespers echoed in our ears:

> *'Who do men say I am, the son of man?'*
> *'I say thou art Christ, son of the living God!'*
> *'And I say to thee that thou art Peter:*
> *On this rock I will build my church.'*

Discussion and more discussion. Then the invasion
Of an army of workmen, pouring into this hollow of the plain
Like its five rivers, and spreading over the countryside.
Directly under me, the men of my own lodge:

Stone-cutters, carvers in freestone, wallers and setters;
And continually behind us, feeding us from the quarry,
The rough hewers of the stone, haulers and carters,
Drivers of twelve-ox wagons; and those who supplied us
With sand and timber, and draughts of morning ale!
And at our heels again, the joiners and carpenters,
Wood-carvers, slatters, plumbers and glaziers,
Each with his knot of apprentices and pride in craft—
Not forgetting the Treasurer who quarried for gold
In the pouches of the wealthy, and the Cathedral Steward
Who minted it in smaller coin to pay our wages.
And Master Jocelyn, of course, Master Jocelyn,
Who drew his skirts from our dust, yet fussed around us,
Inspecting and questioning, before reporting to the Chapter,
Like a hen who scratches importantly and withdraws to peck.

VI

Ah, but once begun, even he
Could not disturb my peace. How should he?
Why, even a hairshirt monk, who harbours
A colony of ardent fleas, performs his rites
With soul unbitten. Why not I
With my solitary louse? . . . So I scratched, but smiled.

Then, in a flood, all my original delight
Returned. I accepted the limitations he imposed,
Absorbed them in my conception. And as you know—
In poetry the same—a creative mind can thrive
On limitations. The challenge of a prescribed form
Calls out some further strength, almost creating
The words that can subdue it, till it becomes
Servant not master. True, I have regretted
The spire and bay-design, but not enough
To maim my pleasure. Besides, what consolations!
Which? Those shafts of smooth, grey Purbeck
That round each sandstone pier? They are much admired.
I love them too. So tall, so slender. . . .

Stolen from Worcester, of course. No cathedral,
Like Zeus, is self-begotten. I could talk for hours
On the heredity of art. (I won't, I promise you!) The virtue
Is not to refrain from stealing, but to steal with judgment,
Shaping to our own needs, and improving on it
As I have done. There are none—none like them
In the whole span of Europe—standing there
In fours and eights around their central pillars,
As girls, in Maytime, stand marshalled for the dance.

And so much more. Look!—look around you
And above! Everything, from the humblest plinth
To the loftiest boss-pinned heaven of the vault—all
Is instinct with love, the God-within-the-stone!
There—I repeat myself. I am growing old.
I have given my years to her. But confess, sir—
Is she not worth it, this living creature
I've played the midwife to? Is she not beautiful?

VII

A Cathedral is more than the stones composing her. She is
The cave and the temple—descendant of all experiments
That man has made, to shelter in one space
His body and his soul. . . . She is the thoughts
Of those who conceived her, the skill and sweat
Of her craftsmen. She is more. She is the patina
Of time upon her surface, the rubbing of wind and weather.
She is the pilgrims who pray there, the line of visitors
Who gape and stare, not knowing at what
They stare. She is decay and reconstruction.
She is beauty, courage, endurance. She is epitome
Of all that we have loved, all we have attained
In our search for the unattainable. . . . Until
That final doom awaits all man's creations,
By man's own hand, or Nature's retaliation,
She is herself: she is the Cathedral.

26

Ballad of the Bishop's Trees

*A legend told in the sixteenth century
of a happening in the thirteenth*

Now listen well to the tale I tell,
   And mark what I do sing,
For you shall be told of a Bishop bold
And how he tricked a King.

The Bishop he came to the King's palace
And humbly bent his knee.
'What are your tidings, my Lord Bishop?
What boon do you crave of me?'

'I build a church in Dorbury, sire,
For the glory of God and thee;
But gold is scarce and timber too,
We lack for many a tree.'

'No gold have I, my good Lord Bishop,
No gold have I to spare,
But yet is many a stout oak tree
Grows in my forest there.

'O you may take for the Church's sake
As many within my park
As may be felled in three full days
Between the dawn and dark.'

The Bishop thanked the King right well,
Though he smiled upon the side;
And he is away to the West again
As fast as he may ride.

And when he came to his own palace
To sit in the Bishop's hall,
He summoned to him an hundred priests
And called his tenants all.

'Three days the King has granted us
To hew what wood we may.
Tomorrow we leave for the royal Chace
Before the dawn of day!

'Go rouse your friends, good neighbours all,
Go rouse them every one,
And bid them meet and greet us there
At the rising of the sun.

'For whoso comes to the Church's aid
Shall be pardoned for all his pain;
But whoso stays to his own labour
No blessing shall he gain.

'And hearken now: both stick and bough
Shall lie on the forest paths
For all who come to bear them home
To feed their winter hearths.'

Next day they came to Dorbury Chace
With a hundred men beside,
From far and near, with rope and gear
And axes true and tried.

The Bishop chose the fairest oaks
Of all those forest trees.
'By Peter's shrine, this mark is mine—
In God's name claim I these!'

His axemen stood in the leafy wood,
They made the forest ring,
And oaktrees all as fast did fall
As corn at harvesting.

'Now who shall stay to cut?' they asked,
'And who away shall come?
For half may lop the branches off,
And half may bear them home.'

'Nay, let them bide!' the Bishop cried,
And held his sides for laughter.
'The word says *felled* in three full days:
Let hauling follow after!'

With strength renewed, they hacked and hewed
Till ne'er an oak did stand;
And they builded a church on Dorbury Meads,
The fairest in the land.

Now when they told the King of this,
He frowned, and then did smile.
'Now who would have thought my little Bishop
To be so full of guile!

'But I forgive the holy man,
If the church is builded well,
That St Peter may my sins forgive
And save my soul from Hell.

'But if that Bishop comes again
To seek our royal grace,
He'll get but a twig and a sparrow's egg
From out of Dorbury Chace!'

Stone-Carver

THIRTEENTH CENTURY

THESE carvings between cloister and chapterhouse?—when
    were they started?
You might ask when a flower started, the beginnings
Of a song or a marriage. Was it the first note struck,
And the last dragging word at the nuptial supper?
Or should we return to the singer's earliest ballad—
Lute-strings answering his mood at their own playing?—
A glance across the rose-hedge in an evening garden?
Before that, surely, to the child's solitary chanting,
The first propensity for love in the apprentice heart.

And so with sculpture: it is less creation
Than a reassembling of the before-created, a melting
Down of memories in the unpredictable instant
When some spark, through the unguarded senses, catches
The mind alight, and all is a chaos of seething
Impressions, which the artist's concentration moulds
Before the whole mass hardens. Yet the spark itself
Is the only new element—that is the yeast
Which sets the flat dough rising.

These carvings then: to find their source
I'd need to wander through a labyrinth of beginnings
Each leading to an earlier recollection.
But take what seems the first path first:
Henry Falcon. He was the Master Mason
When our Cathedral was building. After my father took me
And signed my bonds, Falcon set me working
In the long penthouse behind the eastern end.
For five years I breathed stone-dust,

Shuffled in stone-dust, carrying squares and templates
From draughting-board to work-bench; checking tools
And counting them at night-fall—mallets, stone-saws,
Drills and chisels; hauling the chain-tackle
To raise the tremendous blocks, or greasing boards
That slid them to the next workman. Then I learned
To use these tools myself, how to dress the stone
And polish to mirrors the shafts of Purbeck marble
That rose in clusters round the white columns;
How to cut the rough cone that formed the capitals
For some carver to fashion into leaf or cornsheaf,
Or a monk with tooth-ache. At once I knew: 'This—
This is my work—and nothing in the world else!'

Well, that was one beginning. I became a lover—
That's the only way to work—yes, and a jealous one,
Hating to see the virgin stone violated
By other hands—by men whose only ambition
Was to copy and re-copy the patterns they had seen
In their 'prentice days, with no spark of themselves added,
No observation.—Men who had never watched a hedgehog
Shamble pathetically across a lane, cutting one
In stone, and thinking (if they thought at all) that theirs
Was its equal. Why, those were not births of art,
But the monsters of in-breeding. 'When I'm a sculptor,'
I told myself, 'I'll not attempt to carve
The block into a rose. I'll let the flower
Blossom from the stone.' So at the next stage
In the Master's workshop, studying geometry and drawing,
Preparing designs, and working at cones myself
Under his direction, I tried to combine the formal
With the actual—to see each separate pattern
Part of the building, yet part of nature too;
So that a crouching rabbit, that lent its ears
To the curve from pier to arch, at the same wild moment
Heard the squared reapers closing in. . . .

31

Words on my ears like blows.—Falcon
Stopped at my bench, rebuked me, and walked on.
But later, when the others left, returning moodily
He looked again—more at myself, I think,
Than at my rabbit—questioned me kindly, and my thoughts,
Dammed for so long by my inward brooding,
Came flooding out. He said little then, but afterwards
He halted often, suggesting more moulding here,
Less undercutting there, criticising my work
Less for its nonconformity to the teacher's rules
Than to my own ideals. Sometimes I'd think:
'The Chapter-house and the Cloister-passage—suppose
When their turn comes—suppose. . . .' If asked a motif,
What would I choose?

                  Then—my next beginning—
In a cornfield one afternoon, watching the poppies
As they swayed in the harvest breeze, a peasant stopped me.
We talked of corn and poppies, and she told me,
Learning my trade, she hated the Cathedral—guess!—
For the million buttercups it blotted out. . . .
Yes, you may laugh and think her mad, but to me
That meeting was revelation, an act of God.
There was my motif—gildcup petals opening
To the sun. The Church would repay her stolen flowers
With my perennials!

                  That night, the Master
Called me at candlelight—sharp-featured, billed
Like a falcon—studied me as one unknown, and then:
'I'm sending you to Rheims. A new spirit is alive
In Europe. Men are looking now past Universals
To the nature of the individual. Philosophy
Moves that way, and art will follow. It's a conception
I understand, but cannot rise to in my work.
To you, as your face reveals, the theory's nothing,

But already, unless I'm much mistaken, your eyes
And hands know it. Go to Rheims.
Go with clean vellum and a clear mind.
See and draw. But mostly feel. Yes,
And laugh a little: get buoyancy, gaiety
Behind your chisel. Go to France and find it.'

And there at Rheims, on the wall of the West Front
Above John Baptist, I saw my buttercups
Clustered like lilies on a pond, and behind him
An exquisite panel of their leaves. At first, wonder;
Then respect for craft; finally despair.
For all my aspirations were figured there—
What was there left to do? I made my drawings,
And travelled to Chartres and the Sainte Chapelle.
Everywhere, in the new work, the same story:
Oakleaves, vineleaves, leaves of every sort
Carved with the same assurance, the same perfection
Of insight, as if the very world were created new,
For us, the first Adam, to see and marvel at.
Even twilight songs I heard in the vineyards,
In the cornfields of Provence, held this joyousness,
This life-wonder. Yes, one I remember:

> *Buds break and birds are singing,*
> *Gildcups shine in the green grass;*
> *In watermeadows, where larks are winging,*
> *I sigh to see my Lady pass.*

Who could be young and hear such songs in the springtime
And not be happy? So, under their influence,
My despair faded. Though ambition was killed,
Life was alive here—and I lived and drew.

But as my notebook and my roll of drawings fattened,
Till I'd tossed all else from my pack, I began to notice
The differences within their unity. The individual hand
That carved the leaves added some fragment of itself,

The craftsman's signature. Then gradually I realised
That art can never end—not while the Creator
Shapes every creature new, and gives new eyes
To each beholder. Now, my mission ended,
I stood on the shores of France; and across the waves
Saw the half-formed Cathedral on the clouds.
My beginnings were over. Now I could begin.

Gargoyles

CROUCH we and leer from our quoin of the guttering,
And rain in our jowls goes a-gurgling and spluttering.

'Splodge be my name!'—'Splurge be mine!'—
Thus we squat, come foul, come fine.

Drought in the city, drought on the plain:
Dry lips gaping, we thirst for rain.

'Splurge, be watching?'—'Splodge, be hearkening?'—
'Thunder are rolling'—'Clouds do be darkening.'

First but a licking, a spittling, a tickling,
Then on to our gums the rain comes trickling.

'Splodge, be gladsome?'—'Ay, that I be:
Sky-water, Splurge, be the dose for we!'

Down they roof and along them spout,
Sliding and streaming it oozes out.

Hark on the leads to the pitter-patter
Where a million cloud-drops spill and spatter!

And as on our backs the floods be a-dashing,
Our mouth-jets into the earth go splashing.

'Storm do be heavier!'—'Stream do be stronger!'—
Our chops get fuller and our squirt gets longer!

And ah, what joy! and oh, what wonder!
To spit on the church-men scattering under!

Dean and canons go scampering by,
Sheltering pates from the leaking sky;

But Splodge and Splurge have nought to fear—
High hob-goblins what hob-nob here!

Wandering Scholars

HERE to your church we've come—
Scholars of Christendom

From Gascony, Normandy,
Brittany, Lombardy,

Ireland and Italy,
Tuscany, Sicily—

To match you in rhetoric,
Wenching or Arabic!—

Quoting from Sophocles,
Plato and Socrates,

Proving erroneous
Much of Plutonius,

35

Mixing theology,
Wine and philology,

Letting Divinity
Hoodwink virginity,

Repeating the triple-kissed
Words of the Lutanist:

> *Life's a short journey;*
> *Life is a flower*
> *That wakes with the morning*
> *And dies with the hour.*

Dry-as-dust scholarship
Not for this fellowship!

Down with all masters who
Think the bare bones will do!

We want the blood of it,
The pulse and the flood of it:

Not pluses and minuses
To say who Aquinas is!

Words from the mind alone
Like leaves to the wind are blown:

Heart with the head must lie,
Each in the other die,

Ere lean Philosophy
Begets Truth or Poetry.

Out from the scholars' tomb!
Follow the man in whom

Pagan and Christian meet—
He of the Paraclete!

Ah, God in his mercy guard
The soul of Pierre Abelard,

Bring him, with words like these,
Home to his Heloise:

> *Life is a blossom,*
> *A flower in the sun.*
> *Oh, take the bee now*
> *Ere the summer is done.*

Victim of treachery
After sweet lechery,

Still for the truth he went,
Virile in argument.

Men deemed it privilege
To come to his hermitage,

And though the fields swallowed him,
All Paris followed him!

So to your church we come,
Scholars of Christendom,

To debate with the best of you,
Love with the rest of you,

Singing the night away
With carol and roundelay,

And all the delights that bring
Solace to wandering:

> *Life is a flower*
> *That leaves us behind;*
> *It falls like a petal,*
> *A leaf in the wind.*

Crusader

THIRTEENTH CENTURY

The Voices

Cathedral Guide
William Longespée the Second
His father, the first Earl
His mother, the Countess Ela
His standard-bearer, Robert de Vere
Robert of Artois, brother to Louis of France
William de Sonnac, Master of the Templars.

*

GUIDE:

Now this tomb, which is almost unique,
Is that of William Longespée the Second,
Son of the Earl whose assumed grave
We have just inspected . . .

FIRST EARL:

Half-brother to the King,
Sheriff of this County, Lieutenant of Gascony,
Flos Comitum!

38

GUIDE:

>   . . . Not strictly his tomb,
> Because the man died, or more correctly
> Was killed, in the year twelve-fifty
> Or thereabouts, in Syria, and was buried
> If buried at all, in the church at Acre,
> The Church of the Holy Cross . . .

LONGESPÉE:

>   He ceased
> To breathe and be: the sword-stroke
> Knew its mind. Cleaving the mail
> Like so much lace-work, despite the chainhood
> Wimpling my neck, it pierced my throat
> At the arm's juncture. Ah, instantly
> For doom I knew it—clutched my pommel—
> Rose rigidly in saddle—saw
> Far below, on his dream-horse, a man
> Crying as he fell: 'Too soon!
> Nay, God—too soon!'
> Grossly mistaken. Late enough
> In his fate's reckoning.

STANDARD BEARER:

>   Two hundred knights
> Rode with him—I, Robert de Vere,
> Bearing the arms of England and Anjou.
> After the Bishop's blessing at the altar,
> We'd sailed for Egypt, answering the call
> Of Louis, Saint of France. Courteously
> He received us, and graciously, as befitted
> A King's nephew. But his brother there,
> The Devil's bastard, Robert of Artois,
> He from the first, with his French arrogance,
> Sought to embroil us, mocking my lord,

39

Dubbing him 'Long-tail'—ay, and ourselves
'The long-tailed English'. He, Longespée,
Forbearing to quarrel, swore in truth
He would not be deterred from pagan foe
By Christian braggart. Still they taunted us,
And many a time, though his hand itched,
He held his counsel. So campaigned together
These friends most deadly. At Mansurât
—While Artois halted, his armies useless—
We routed caravans, taking their gold
And spice and other plunder, which Artois,
Ever with the ear of the French King,
Afterwards seized. We had slain them gladly,
These mincing thieves with their brave manners,
But my lord forebade. 'Nay,' said he,
'It is not our King's purpose.' But then,
Fearless yet without anger, to their King
He spoke, and in these words rebuked him:

LONGESPÉE:

If thou, sire, canst not urge thy knights
To Christian humility nor pagan valour,
Saint thou mayst be, but King
Assuredly thou art not.

STANDARD-BEARER:

At this,
Such was his mien, though many rose,
None dared to touch him. We passed
Out of the King's tent, and towards Syria
Rode with our English host. Later
We returned, Louis having for service
William de Sonnac, an honest man,
He who was then Master of Templars
And of all knights first in Christendom.
Artois greeted us:

ARTOIS:

              Ah, I see,
The English have returned, given new heart
By Sonnac's reinforcements!

DE SONNAC:

              They acquitted themselves
Valiantly, and their presence here
Is now most welcome. The infidels are there,
See!—gathered in the Nile's arms.
Louis, our brother, having crossed the river,
Will join us here. Let us wait his coming.

LONGESPÉE:

Such is my counsel, too. If we wait
Success is certain.

ARTOIS:

             The only glory
Lies in uncertainty—wrestling nobly
And conquering against odds. I see:
The English are afraid.

LONGESPÉE:

            This is too much!

DE SONNAC:

Peace, my Lord, he is not worth
Your anger. Think. Do not sacrifice
To cheap taunts the cause of Christendom.

ARTOIS:

The long-tailed English are afraid.

LONGESPÉE:

By Christ!
I have stood enough. I tell you, Artois—
I will ride this day where not you,
No, nor your damned Frenchmen, the dregs
Of chivalry, will dare draw level
With my horse's tail!

STANDARD-BEARER:

So saying,
He turned, motioning to hold aloft
The Lion-banner. With a great cry
The English mounted, formed their lines,
And following, set spur to flank.
Horses' wild eyes, sunflash
On shields, cries, hooves' thunder—
And into the shrieking enemies of Christ
We hurled ourselves!

COUNTESS ELA:

I, at that instant,
Seated with my nuns in the high Choir,
Saw his shield on the stalls before me—
Six lions blazing in the sunlight—
And he, my son, in full armour,
I saw him raised into the courts of Heaven
With bands of angels on either hand.

GUIDE:

. . . And as I was saying,
The design of this effigy is noteworthy,
One of the finest examples of its kind.
Notice the surcoat with its long folds;
And under it the elaborate chain-armour—
Literally 'from top to toe'. Also the legs
Crossed at the knees. So much for that.
Now in the next arcade. . . .

Wood-Carver

THIRTEENTH CENTURY

'You carve the misericords—you and John.
     One aside, from this end, and pace each other.'—
That's what the Master said.—'Not race, mind you.
Take your time and give the best that's in you.'
'What's the theme, sir?'—'Noah and the Ark.'
The Ark, I thought. Well, that suits me, I reckon:
All the animals in creation and a few outside it.
No tearing the hair and wondering what to chip.
We'll start our menagerie here by the Choir gangway,
March 'em down two-by-two, and next year
Bring them to their Ararat under the East Window. . . .
'Remember the window-lighting—its effect on contours.'
'Ay, sir—we will that, and thank you, sir.'
'Why "misericords"?' asked John, puzzled,
After the Master left. 'Why not?' I told him,
'They'll cause us misery enough before we've finished.
Come on—stop gawping, and hunt the brutes!'

So around the Choir we went, squatting and squinting,
Turning this way and that, with head on one side
Like a robin or a wry-necked zany in the porch,
Grovelling on all fours like beasts ourselves,
To study shapes, the run of the grain, and see
Noah's family arked in the rough wood
Waiting for us to carve them out again.—
Like the story they tell in Wales, of a spirit prisoned
For centuries in the tight bole of an oak
Till some magician, unsaying the spell, released him.

Next day we started sketching them in charcoal,
Wrist-strokes following the line of the tree.
Then, working swiftly with our largest gouges,
We roughed out masses to get a broad effect.

Later chisel and mallet to pare these down
And feel the strength of shadow, with figures hovering
In the wood, the magician's spell half-said.
And last of all, using our lightest mallets
Or pushing with palm of hand, we freed them,
Acting as midwife to each new birth.—
Yet not wholly free, for we kept a connection
With the seat itself, a sort of navel-cord
Binding it to the mother tree; so that watching
That blundering horde of beasts, however varied,
You see them all belonging to a single breed:
Bastards who know their common parent—wood.

Holy Mary! but what a brood they are!
Bears, gryphons, leopards and unicorns—
Every animal under the sun or moon—
Loping eastward before the first rain falls:
Some with their eye over a troubled shoulder,
Fearful lest one panting from the stall behind
Outdistance them—though he won't, God willing,
Not in a thousand years.—One hound, carefree,
Stopping to mate by the way, a monstrous joy
On his snout; and a fox, hen in mouth,
Bringing his larder with him—one the less
For Noah's tally!

    . . . So we went on,
Old John and me, coming across at meal-breaks
To see the other's work, joking about it,
Complaining of the length of a faun's tail,
Or the way a hind leg bent in running.
But knowing in our hearts, as the Master did,
We matched each other.—Ay, and knowing too
Had his been poorer work, our own had suffered.
Summer and winter passed: sunlight, snowlight.
And all was done—all save the two leggèd
Fussing and quarrelling around the Ark itself.

Now they are here. Ham, Shem and Japhet
Argue as to a cubit's length, plane planks
And drive in pegs. Their three wives,
Counting fruit and flour-sacks with Mrs Noah,
Bicker about their quarters, hold noses
And point distastefully at the gibbering monkeys.
Noah, disquieted, doubting a quiet voyage,
Stands apart, a choir-stall to himself. His eyes
Search the sunrise. Rainwind ruffles his hair.
One gnarled hand, to comfort him,
Caresses the soft dove. Our mates and wives
Have taken turns as models—though they may not know it.
And Noah? Who but the old Bishop himself,
No chin worth chiselling and the longest nose in Christendom!

Today, the first of Spring, he came to see them.
Blackthorns were breaking in the fields outside
And birds clamorous with their own building
As the Master brought him. He smiled indulgently
At our cheerful monsters; smiled slyly at Japhet
Posing there with the Master's very stance
And the Master's angry frown when measuring.
'That face is familiar,' he said, 'vaguely familiar.
I guess he keeps order among his lesser brethren.'
And chuckled softly. But at Father Noah
He shook his head. 'Ah no; not quite,
Not quite. A thinker—administrator perhaps—
But not the religious type. Would Almighty God
Trouble to save *him* from a watery end?
I doubt it. I very much doubt it.
Ah, never mind: the rest redeem him.
I do congratulate you. The finest beasts
This side of Creation—and, in my opinion,
Infinitely preferable to those at York.'

Corpus Christi Play

THIRTEENTH CENTURY

(Directions to Players)

'A PARADISE is to be built on a raised platform
Before the West Door, with curtains of silk
Beneath it. Fragrant flowers and leaves
May be set closely therein, and divers trees
Laden with hanging fruit, all giving likeness
To a most delicate garden. Then from the Cathedral
Shall the Saviour come, crossing the greensward.
Now let Adam and Eve be brought to the Figure
And stand before him, reverend, yet composed in countenance,
While he instructs them in their several duties
And leads them to Paradise. . . .

                        When he hath gone,
And they in the orchard of Paradise walk in delight,
Let demons run about the stage invisible,
Making suitable gestures, motioning to the fruit.
Then cometh the Devil in person to dispute with Adam,
But he, remembering his Creator, rebuketh him.
Whereat the Devil, much put out of countenance,
With downcast gaze going to the mouth of Hell,
Holds earnest council with his fellow demons
How to gain power over the man and the woman.
Then shall he make a sally amongst the beholders,
And return from the other side, approaching Eve.
By the tree he shall converse with her, subtle,
Insinuating, promising all manner delight.
At first she refuseth him, but from the tree's trunk
Shall rise a Serpent most cunningly contrived,
Who breathing in her ear shall melt her will.
She taketh the apple now. She giveth it to Adam,
Who eateth part thereof, and straightway repenteth.
He abaseth himself, and putting on solemn raiment,

46

(Let it be poor apparel sewn of fig-leaves),
With an air of dolour falleth to lamentation.
Again from the Cathedral let the Figure come,
Pacing and majestic. . . . At his command
An Angel appeareth, bearing a flaming sword,
Who, when they have departed, guardeth the gate.

Eve shall take her a hoe, and Adam a spade,
And together they shall make to till and sow;
But let the Devil arising plant thorn and thistle,
So that they, seeing the fruits of their labour,
May be smitten with grief and loudly beat their breasts.
Then let the Devil, with four demons,
Put fetters and chains about their feet and necks
And draw them Hellwards. From the fiery mouth
Bring forth other demons for high revel.
Now shall Eve and Adam be seized with roughness
And cast into Hell's Mouth. Let those behind
Cause a great smoke to arise, and call aloud,
And clash their pots and kettles, while other devils
Shall hold the stage and dance upon their toes.'

Martyr

No, do not pity me. It came swiftly
   To my very altar—not lingering death
From age or fever, when gross indignities
Of body debilitate the mind, and the spirit's passion
Dwindles to a creed, or to petulant fumbling
Of rosaries between the fingers.—I,
When fully I, saw Death before me,
And grasping his sword between my two hands
Drew it towards my heart.
Nor call it sacrifice. I willed the event

47

Deliberately as I ruled my people here
And half this kingdom. The great administrator
Ordered his end—and like a palace servant
Death must obey him. For this martyrdom
Was my spirit's consummation. Through my life
That was my guiding star. All else—
Men's wishes, reason, my own comfort
And promptings of the flesh, even ambition,
Were bent to that purpose, and if they resisted
Broken. . . . Was that sacrifice?
Was Christ's, my master's, when he journeyed
Through prophecies to his tree, and he himself
Did all but drive the nails?
If that is sacrifice, it is a free offering
Of man on his own soul's altar;
Losing for gain; giving the world for heaven,
Time for Eternity. . . . What merit,
Exchanging for a gold crown a copper farthing?
So do not worship me, seeking my shrine
Of jewels and silver, wearing the steps away
With suppliant knee. All these will pass
Like dew before the sun. There is only one
Merits your worship—he who forged the world
Under its canopy of stars—only he
Worthy of worship. I, for all my will,
For all the power, ruthlessness and adulation
Am but a drop in that vast and shoreless sea.

Spire-Builder

FOURTEENTH CENTURY

At the angle of the Bishop's palace,
Where the yew-tree throws its shade

And autumn needles on the grass,
I stood transfixed,
As a saint, heart-stopped,
Might listen to the voice of God,
For there, in my mind's vision
(Though clear as truth it cut
The sky above the meadows)
I saw it. . . . The spire!

Five years, as master-mason,
I had lived with the Cathedral,
Known its moods, as a countryman
The seasons, felt its presence
A living thing; as a child
To its mother is a warm life,
A thing that breathes and grows.
I came, too, to experience
The creative mind within,
That which a century before
Conceived and fashioned it.
Guarding the stone, watchful
For decay or subsidence,
I learned to know his mind,
Followed it through the act of Becoming—
As when, in the great moments
Of any art (listening
To music, perhaps, or poetry)
The interpreter becomes the artist,
And we feel upon our own flesh
The shiver of creation.
So I followed him. But the end,
When I reached there, was not
The end; the Cathedral was unfinished.
Seeing it from the North East—
Its massing, the magnificent grouping
Of transepts and Lady Chapel—

Kindled one's expectation
Only to disappoint:
A low central tower
As squat as Westminster's—
The church flattening the meadows
Instead of rising from them—
The pinnacles crying for a spire
To cap them. In my imagination
A hundred lifted to the sun
And were demolished. And then,
As I have told you, I saw it.
As though he, not I, were standing there
I saw it—and I knew.

How to build it, that
Was the problem, how to support
On four delicate piers
Of Chilmark stone with their flutings
Of Purbeck marble, that spire
(Six thousand tons in weight)
Which in his dreams and mine
Rose with such sureness to the clouds?
All my training declared
Against it; Canons came
And wagged their tonsures at me;
And I watched, in sleepless nights,
My reputation topple. . . .
Then I began to build.
Buttresses I set flying
From the four angles of the tower
To take the colossal out-thrust;
The spire casing I pared
To nine inches. And at her apex,
Nearest to heaven and the winds,
We placed in a relic box
A fragment of St Peter's robe.
And finally, though it seemed mistrustful

Of the saint's protection, we left
Inside the cone, the framework
Standing, the crisscross scaffolding
Of seasoned oak. Then
If the impossible occurred, and the spire
In her precarious beauty survived
The centuries that stormed about her,
That would be miracle enough!

Often, on summer evenings,
(In my autumn days) I stand
By this yew-tree, and see my vision
Made permanent on the sky,
Her living grey a foil
To every light that comes. As I watch,
And she stirs and rises from the meadows
As a spirit rises, moving
To the background of moving clouds,
My love goes out to her,
And all my evening prayers.

The People

THIRTEENTH–FOURTEENTH CENTURIES

WE, too, the people of England,
    Have built this Cathedral—men and women
Who know little of the making of beauty
But who, when beauty comes, can feel
Its presence—can find in their troubled lives
An anchorage, a haven, a calm assurance
Of something greater and beyond themselves
Which, though they die, survives.

*The *Peasant* toiling on his fifteen acres,
Ploughing, sowing, harrowing, reaping;
Labouring three days for the manor-lord
With boon-work at harvest. *His *Wife*,
Who rears in the same hovel his hens and his children,
Cards and spins for the lord's steward
And sells her eggs at the Thursday market.
Fishermen from villages of the South West,
Smoothing into port after the churning and blustering
Sea, dragging their catch up the beach
And spreading nets on the dry rocks.
Manor Lady, discussing with her sempstress
The fashionable gown-length, and whether
One shield or two should be embroidered on the shoulder.
*'Yes, to compass men's praise
You spend much labour on your apparel,
Your veils and your kirtles. Indeed, the making
Is more costly than the cloth itself,
With your tucks and flouncings around the hem.
Not only do you take pride in your buttonholes:
You plague your feet with exquisite torments,
Trotting this way and that with your fine stitching.
You busy yourself with unnecessary veils—
You twitch them here and twitch them there,
And even as you pretend to listen to my sermon
Your thoughts are on the new hairstyle.'
*The *Baker*, who bakes his customers' flour
And removes two ounces in every twelve
Under their very noses. *'Here he comes now,
Dragged through the streets on a bouncing hurdle
As a remembrancer to the trade!' *Fairweather sailor,
Horse dealer, horse-stealer,
Roaring like a sea-lion at Dorbury Fair,
Jostling and badgering with his pedigree words.
He steers through the crowd his nags and colts,
Packhorses and carthorses, keeping to windward

*A different voice takes up.

The blind eye and the spavined flank.
*City Merchant, displaying in his shop
Fruits from the Levant, silks from Damascus,
Drugs and spices from Alexandria,
Brought by armed galley through Genoa
And the ports of Venice. *Schoolboys
Loosed like arrows on holy-days,
Giving to football, wrestling, cock-throwing
A devotion seldom accorded to their Latin.—
*'Now if you please, lads—outside,
No games allowed in the Cathedral Close,
Plenty of fields beyond.' *—homing
Like cattle at feeding-time, falling to bed
With full bellies and a sleep without conscience.
*Merchant's Wife, bustling about her kitchen
Preparing conserves and sweetmeats, tending
Her herb-garden, and making sweet concoctions
Of scented flower-water. *Wise-Woman
Who lives at the last cottage on the Plain.
She, also, has an interest in herbs.
She brews them into the most potent remedies
Against scurvy, empetigo and love-sickness,
Or with equal ease and efficiency
Creates these disorders where they do not exist,
For a hard word spoken or a contemptuous glance,
And helps your cattle to wither in their stalls.
*Archers practising for the Welsh campaign
Under the yew-trees in Dorbury Close.
'Draw to ear!—mark!—release!'—
The target pierced at two hundred paces.
*The Chapman, trudging country lanes,
With an old horse that halts before each village
To pluck at the thick, lush grasses
While his master eases and evens the pack-weight
And blows dust from shoulder-trays.
*'Come! buy! Ribbons and purses,

* A different voice takes up.

Keen knives, scarves and kerchiefs,
Buckles and trinkets-O! Come buy!'
Masters, journeymen and seven-year '*prentices*,
Following their crafts in gold and silver,
Steel-work, leather-work—maintaining the honour
Of their guilds.—Some rising to Aldermen,
Strutting majestically in scarlet processions,
Stretching majestically on tombs.

All these, thronging the Western shires,
Have built the Cathedral—from guild-merchant
In eager counting-house to the widow
Clutching her lonely penny. These,
Working and giving, though giving reluctantly
Or with the wrong motive, have built this Cathedral.
Their thoughts and hopes have fed its walls,
Impregnated the stone, are part
Of its atmosphere. Though dead, long
Dead, we still survive, one
With its continuity, the common heritage.

Vespers

FOURTEENTH CENTURY

So vast a gloom in the vast Cathedral
As night falls, the December night.
Slowly, inevitably, it unbuilds
The Cathedral. Already the vaulted roof
Has gone, the leaning Angel with her trumpet
Of triumphant gold. Carvings on capitals
Sink back into the crude stone.

* A different voice takes up.

Broken columns rise from shadow
Into shadow. Night covers
The stretched and bloodless windows with a pall
Of dusk. One flame, trembling
At the end of the long riding, burns
Like a cottager's lamp between shafts of trees.
For the shadows are a wood's shadows, when clouds
Have curtained the moon. . . .

High in the gloom a bell rings,
Gabriel, the storm-bell—so clear
Through the thick of night, the note shivers
In that great room, as if the darkness knew
The threatened music of the bells would sound
Its doom. Another, another joins it:
Margaret, high and sweet, like morning,
Like a morning in May. Now from the shadows
Figures loom, bearing the light
And smell of tapers. One by one,
At the high altar, shine wavering
Stars, and round the Martyr's tomb.
James, John and Michael add
To the bells' clamour. Columns return
With their smooth Purbeck stems, with opening
Leaf and flower, while candles bloom
At fifteen altars. The procession forms.
Then Peter, in his tower, booms out
His message to the world, and all the bells
With a last thunderous clapping proclaim
The death of Night. The procession moves.
And the choir, the golden Angel in the roof—
Ave, rex gentis Anglorum—
Take up the luminous theme of light.

Pilgrim

FOURTEENTH CENTURY

FRO wyf and lond, withouten moore abood,
On a May morwê to Dorbury I rood,
That by the chirche's seint, Peter of Rome,
I myghte fynde conforte in my hertê's home.
I sette my hors, as soon as sonne gan shyne,
Thrugh lanes of hawethorn and of eglentyne,
But tho it happed ful twentie yeares behynd,
The synne I bore lay heavie on my mynd,
Soe that ne bud ne blossyme did I see
Of alle the floures that bursten on the tree.
For two long deyes its ymage did me keepe,
And thrugh the nyght it prisounded me fro slepe.

Thanne on the evenyng of the secound deye
I met a band of pylgrimes by the weye,
Who laughed and talked and jangled on the reyne
As if they rood for plesaunce, not for peyne.
They toulde of robberes hidyng in the woode
To lighten traveleres of purs and blud,
And of thir felawshipe invited mee
To take my journie in thir campaygnie.
Mo to escape the thoghtês in my head
Thanne theves in woode, I ventured as they seyd.
I laughed with hem and toulde hem merye tales
Of poets, lovyeres, nyghts and nyghtyngales,
Till you hadde thoghte that in the worldê wyde
Ne wyght mo gaie ne shriven e'er did ryde;
And attê taverne where we took oure reste,
I fel to bedde and snoren with the beste.

Thereafter did swich tapestries unfolde
Of orchard, forest and the oupen wolde,

56

Thatte as I ronge the brydel, laught and spoke,
I felt my yeeres downfallen lyk a cloke.
Meseemed the same man, yonge and prosperynge,
Who first that weye hadde wenden in the sprynge.

Soe rood we ful fyve deyes, til sodeynly
We saugh far offe the toure of Dorbury
Uprysyng lyk a speare. It strooke my hertè.
My soulès lyf was wounden with the smertè.
I hadde ne wordès mo. They seyd farewel
And went hir weyes with freende or hooste to dwel,
Swearing, with Goddès blessyng on hir steye,
To meet ageyn upon the homeward weye.
But I, allone as born, within the gate
Tethered my hors for all that it was late,
And, as he croppéd at the grasses tall,
Stoode stil as any shadowe by the walle;
Until I heard Great Peter in his toure
Shake all the nyght with telling of the houre,
Lyke drum of doome. Thanne soghte I out the doore
Wherein I entered twentie yeeres before.

'Long since,' one answered mee, 'she went fro heere.
A child she bore. It dyed within the yeere.'
'And Goddès will it were,' another seyd;
'Ne housbonde refte her of hir maydenhed.
She went into the Convent of Seint Clare
To take hir vowes and mak atonement ther.
But if content, good sir, with swich a thyng,
We are ryght glad to give you harberyng.'

That nyght within the roome where we had leyd
I lay ageyn, and long and long I preyed.
But of soccóur and tendres had I nonne,
Nor slepe came never til the risyng sonne.
My hors I fed, and whenas Prime was songe
To the Cathedral chirche I took my wronge.

At chancel arch I made confessioune,
And by the preste hadde absolutioune.
Thanne knelt I by the shrine where Peter's boune
Of litel finger lyeth on the stoune,
And preyed the seint that as he was forgiven
His Lorde denying, so myght I be shriven.
Whan I had doone, and thoghte my synne had dyed,
I met her eyen by the auter syde.

Knelyng she was, hir wympul whyt and longe,
And rounde hir nek a crucyfysse y-honge
Of Jhesu Crist his ende. Fro chin to brow
Onlie hir eyen showed. That were enow,
Sin that they looked as they did pitie mee
For hir deare Meister's sake. Thanne sodeynly
They sterte with feare. Turning on a breath
I see hir broother, that had sworne my deathe,
Upstanding by the walle. I fynd my feet.
Swiftly along the cloisters to the street
I mak my weye; but ere the doore I win
Am held by presse of pilgrymes comyng in.
I feel his hate behynd. A sodeyn smertè,
And I have dropped, a daggere thurgh my hertè.

Soe, in some planne, by Goddès seint y-roghte,
I founde my peace, but in a different sort.

Travelling Preacher

BYSTANDER:

Mark that mock-priest,
That wandering monk, who
Dressed in his friar's habit
Of brown, road-rusted,
Tonsured and dusty-headed,

Mounts his two-shilling mare
To travel the lanes of England
With neither paper nor parish,
Nor license from the Pope—
Tethering now by that tree
As though at the world's gate.

See how they flock to his words
Like gulls to winter crumbs,
Pouring through cloisters from Mass
To gawp at this tousled prophet,
This uncelled, prowling humbug,
This holy nothing. Say,
Does duty draw them,
Subtle exposition of Scripture?
Or gossip from foreign parts,
Morsels of murder? Listen!
He comes spreading slander,
Engendering discord, dissention,
Exciting peasants' revolt
Under cloak of religious truth.
Sheriff's and king's men,
Showing more diligence,
Should grant him a civic cell,
Rat's room and fetters.

PREACHER:

. . . And so, in the beginning of the world, were neither
Fine clothes nor mighty buildings,
Yet God was there, even in the garden:
His sun shone equally on all creation.
'*When Adam delved and Eve span,*
Who was then the gentleman?'
And who the prelate in rich attire
Eating magnificently the labour of others,
Returning but a few poor chants
And lighted candles? Did our Lord,

The Lord of Heaven, do such things?
When he set his disciples upon their road
To wander as I do, did he not tell them
To take no purse, not even a staff
For the journey, trusting their Father
To know their needs, like birds of the air
Or flowers of the field? Yet these his friends
Were called as equals to the throne of Heaven.

Good people: know your worth.
Our Lord has named you Children of God
As you do his bidding. In his eyes
Are neither serfs nor masters, and I say:
England shall not be worthy of his love
Till this bondage is ended, till all possessions
Are shared for the common good, like Adam's
In Eden, in the springtime of the world.

BYSTANDER:

What? Shall the scoundrel yelp
In our very cloisters? Offer
Blasphemy as grace to Mass?
If Church will not chain him, City
Should seize the dog.—Ay,
Drag him to jail, I say,
Scourge like a truant monk.

The Devil

IN that same year came the Devil to Dorbury
In the guise of a young priest.
He caused much mischief in the refectory,
Where platters flew like birds through the window
And oysters descended on my Lord's head
To his great discomfiture. In the wine-vaults
Bungs were removed from my Lord's casks

In a sad waste of liquor. Yet,
It was noted that this young priest himself
Did neither drink, nor eat, nor sleep,
Which all men marvelled at.
At length, suspecting his strange guest
To be some demon in human form,
My Lord commanded him to be seized
And his holy garments taken from him.
This was performed in the north transept
At Lammastide, by three stout men,
Yet only with great labour did they master him,
And hold him fast to the Bishop's will.
Then, stripped of his frock and most hairy,
He vanished like smoke from between their hands.

Sanctuary

FOURTEENTH CENTURY

By Scanton Market Cross
We each saw each together.
He drove his spur to flank,
I broke my horse from tether.

Though he led by a thousand yards,
I swore there'd be no escaping.
Dust of seven hamlets
We stirred, with the peasants gaping.

Farms once left behind,
The pace of our horses quickened:
Over the Great Plain
We rode as the dusk thickened.

Two, on that vast waste,
Down a road that was white and narrow,

Raced till there rose before us
A spire like a shafted arrow.

Torchlight, we reached the City:
Our hooves on the streets rang hollow.
He left his horse at the gate,
I leapt from mine to follow.

We crossed the darkened Close,
Our spurs on the path clattering.
Torches thrust in our face—
Priests staring and chattering.

One barred our way,
Rebuked us before the Lord—
He for unseemly haste,
I for my drawn sword.

'Sanctuary!' he cried gasping,
And fell in the Choir entry.
The monk gripping my arm
Stood his ground like a sentry.

I sheathed my sword at his bidding,
Removed my cap at another's,
And panting lay in the Porch
Till they fetched their learned brothers.

Thus they agreed: the Chapter,
While he skulked at the High Altar,
Would discuss the pros and cons
And decide by book and psalter.

So, as the talkers talked
And the tapers swayed and blurred,
Prone by Chapter-house wall
I sat in my seat and heard:

Brothers in Christ!
The matter we discuss, that warrants our prayerful attention,
Is no less than a consideration of terms of sanctuary.
But before we give our thoughts to the case before us,
Let us remind ourselves of its place in history.
Sanctuary is not exclusively a Christian custom:
It was known to pagan Rome, also to the temples
Of Greece and Egypt. Its aim, I need hardly remind you,
Is not primarily the preservation of life,
Worthy though that object may be: its roots go deeper.
A man, however dastardly the crime he has committed,
Partakes in degree of that holiness wherein he shelters:
Consequently an assault on his person must be interpreted
As direct and wanton assault on the church itself,
And therefore sacrilege. Roman law at first
Refused to recognise the Christian claim to sanctuary,
But later, towards the end of the fourth century,
Accepted it as a privilege of the Church—a ruling Justinian
Confirmed, and the Edict of Orleans. In England
Its recognition by the Saxon king, Aethelbert,
Brought it acceptance in canon law.

SECOND CANON

Thank you:
An admirable summary of ecclesiastical tradition.
It will be observed, however, that even this law
Admits of considerable difference of interpretation—
Witness the examples quoted by Gregory of Tours.
Now on a practical point I ask your guidance:
Does Sanctuary extend only to the church door,
As is commonly supposed by the vulgar mind,
Or fifty paces beyond?

FIRST CANON

—Valentinian
Decreed it operative even to the outer courtyard—

A dispensation provided to ensure that he,
The victim, if I may so designate him, might eat
And drink, and perform the necessary operations of nature
Outside the sacred precincts.

THIRD CANON

       —Was not that rescinded?
It is now recognised, at least by the law of usage—
Or perhaps I should say by that of disuetude—
That *droit d'asile* reaches not even to the door
But takes effect solely within the walls of the Choir.

FOURTH CANON

In that case, brothers, the condition is now fulfilled;
The man concerned is recumbent in the choir stalls,
Therefore protected.

FIFTH CANON

       —Ah, but protected only
If he makes full confession of his crime, obeys
The rules of our holy Order, and performs penance
Suitably attired.

SIXTH CANON

       —Brothers, excuse me—
A minor point, no doubt—but is it not obligatory
To wear a garment of black cloth, embroidered
With a cross on the left shoulder—or possibly on the right,
My memory is somewhat faulty on detail now. . . .

SEVENTH CANON

Sackcloth seems more appropriate.

EIGHTH CANON

       —Forgive me, brothers,
Before we discuss the material in which he shall live or die,
Would it not be advisable to consider the classifications

Of Sanctuary: conveniently termed General and Chartered?
The first, I understand, applies to all churches,
And admits, as we have seen, of divergent opinions.
The latter is granted by our sovereign Lord
To selected bodies, regulating the punishment of felonies
And applicable to Treason, both High and Petty.

FOURTH CANON

That is indeed most interesting and gratifying.
May I ask if our Foundation has been honoured in this manner?

SECOND CANON

At one time this Cathedral was so chartered, but the wording
Is highly ambiguous. It reads in this fashion:
'Its employment shall be governed by usage within living
    memory.'
And within living memory—unless my brothers'
Extends further than my own—there has been no such usage.
Therefore, I assume, as the rights of charter no longer obtain,
We must regard this case as belonging to the general category,
And base our judgment solely on its merits. . . .

When they gave their final word
The cocks in the town were waking.
'Grace to the Close wall!'—
On the windows dawn was breaking.

Loudly abusing their terms
I left by the North postern;
Piously, in monk's cowl,
Returned at night by the Western.

I watched him venture forth,
Thinking I ceased to pursue him.
In the street where his horse waited
I came behind and slew him.

Candle Carol

For a Children's Procession

To this Cathedral
  Candles we bring
To light the way
To Christ our King.

Down the long aisles
We carry them,
Seeking the Inn
At Bethlehem.

Under the Crossing
The crib we find
That keeps good people
Of Christ in mind.

There Our Lady,
With cloak of blue,
Sits in the stable
All night through.

There St Joseph
Beside her stands,
The hem of her mantle
Between his hands.

There at a hurdle
With wisp of grass,
The Ox looks over
The gentle Ass.

And there on bracken
Before our eyes,
The Lord of Heaven
In manger lies.

Here will we set
Our candles bright,
To praise his coming
This Christmas night.

Long may this church
His glory see,
And may his blessing
Be found by me.

Plague-Pit

UNDER these living leaves, remember,
    These green leaves—here beneath
The smooth green lid of turf
Lies death: Black Death.

Ten feet under, fingered by the elmroots,
Wide as the lurid mouth of hell
Gaped the plague-pit, where they flung
More corpses than were men to tell:—

Cathedral masons, falling from their ladders
As they clutched the unfeeling stone;
Housewives at their ovens; merchants
In crowded inns; shepherds alone;

Travelling Friars, preaching damnation,
Who, halted in mid-sentence, drank
Of the silent air; thoughtless farmgirls
With cheek along the cow's flank;

Children, frozen like legendary children,
With half a smile on their lips, or a boast;
Priests ordained as the last encumbent
Fell at the altar, scattering the Host;

Choirboys, their psalms unfinished;
Canons—whether they stayed or fled—
Lords, ladies, pages, servants,
Beggars and deacons—dead, dead,

Dead—dropping like rotten fruit
In a neglected orchard, lying
Piled up under the trees as they tumbled,
In one heap the dead and the dying.

Those who trembled behind bolted doors,
Or flaunted pageantry and youth and love—
All flung naked into the plague-pit
Hidden by the dead above.

So when, as suddenly, the plague ended,
There were in the city left alive
Of all who breathed and loved and wept,
Only two in every five. . . .

Cover them over now, roll back
The turf whose green life never grieves
For darkened history. The past is past.
Wake to the present world of leaves.

The Reliquary

FIFTEENTH CENTURY

'Drunk, sir? Me? Not a pint I've touched
　　Between sunrise and sundown,
St Peter purge me if I tell a lie.
There!—the sun's in the east window.
Still time if you'll follow me—
Mind that step in the half-light—
And I'll show you the finest relinquy . . .
Relinc . . . Mind your head, sir—
The finest collection of holy relincs
Between Land's End and John o' Gaunt.

Here it is, sir. Wait, wait—
There's a key on this plumbline cord of mine
If I can haul it up. Ah, here it is.
This little bawdy key. So!—
And the door opens. Look there!
Don't touch, sir. 'Kindly requested
Not to handle the holy relincs.'
Now that splinter, that slithering of wood
That looks nothing but a splinter and a slithering,
That was chimped from the True Cross
By St John himself, and brought to England
By Joseph of . . . by St Joseph.
Some clericals, sir, have doubted it,
But our Bishop, he said: 'I declare it
A true and authentical holy relinc.'—
Those were his very words. . . .

Now, you see that piece of rag there?
That was the hair-shirt of poor St Lawrence—
Him they took, sir, and toasted on a gridiron,
Roasted to a martyred steak. See—

69

The very scorch-marks from the bars. Eh?
Why not burned? Because they declared it
A most intolerable holy relinc
And snatched it from him before they basted him,
And that, sir, is a fact. . . . The bone?
Something to do with the Ten Thousand Virgins,
But what it is I've quite forgotten.
I've had no truck with virgins, sir,
Not since I became a lay brother.
But *here's* something—that chomping block.
John the Baptist—Herod. Look!
Still bloodstains down the side.
Tilt your head, sir—the light's going.
Now you see them. . . . I assure you, sir:
Most authentical. 'All relincs here
True and authentical in every disrespect.' . . .
And cures! Not one of these
But owns a miracle, and some a score.
It's a crying shame you're not lame, sir;
Because if you were halted sick
And stuck your legs in these two holes
You'd be a new man from this day forth.
Many's the pilgrim that's stuck them there
And been a new man from that day forth.
No matter, time will tell.
An Inn, sir? The *Golden Lion*—
That's well spoken of, by those who speak well.
The *Bull* takes the singing pilgrims
Who can't hold their liquor. Get there
By nightfall. There's a man by the north gate
Who'd split your skull for the groat in your purse.
Money's a great provoker. Thank you.
Thank you, sir. Most acceplable:
It's sundown, as you say.'

The Clock

FIFTEENTH CENTURY

Two steeds, two riders, stand at gaze:
They stand as Mordred stood
Bewitched, enchanted, held in thrall
In Merlin's magic wood.

Grey or black each halted steed,
With grave, half-lifted head:
One is trapped in cloth-of-gold,
One in green and red.
Their riders wait with spears at rest;
Entranced, each faces other.
Helm and hauberk make them kin;
They might be man and brother.

Neither horse his bridle stirs,
Nor rider stirs his hand.
For sixty minutes by the clock
They haunt their timeless land. . . .

Wheels rumble; steeds tremble;
Then grey horse rears his head
To hear the clock with solemn stroke
Bury the hour that's dead.

Grey knight tilts his lion-shield;
Merlin's spell is done.
Sharply his lance falls, couched to charge;
The herald clock cries 'One'!

The joust begins: with clash of steel
Black lays his pennoned lance.
Gravely, slow, still half in dream,
The battled steeds advance.

They charge: Grey fiercely bears him down,
But Black his lance has swung.
Under his targe, the foeman, struck,
Back on his croup is flung.

The knight recovers, voids and turns,
Spurring his shaken horse.
Round the pavilion both appear
To try a second course.

Again the Grey knight couches lance;
Again he charges Black;
Again with spear to helm is thrown
Full on his horse's back.

He rights himself, and hand on rein,
Wheels for a third assault;
But ere they reach the lists again
Their horses tire and halt.

The chimes have tolled their count of twelve;
Their fading echoes cease.
The tourney ends; foes now are friends;
The clock has sounded peace.

Horses and riders stand at gaze:
The magic word is said.
Each steed is held with hoof upraised
And grave, half-lifted head.

Cure-Seller

FOURTEENTH CENTURY

(*Outside the west door*)

CITIZENS and gentles!—for by your bearing
   I see there be quality among you—
Come! draw near and listen.
My words are not to be shouted from the housetops,
Neither are they to be overheard by the dull-witted. . . .
That is more serviceable. Now, my friends,
I am not one of those miserable preachers,
Nay, nor one of those wretched herbalists
Who stand before this magnificent cathedral
With their starved bodies and threadbare cloaks;
Who, with their boxes spread upon a carpet,
Seek to extract your hard-earned wages.
Know you that I am none of that tribe.
I am sent here by Madame Trote of Salerno,
Who indeed is the wisest woman in the world,
A virgin of most profound sagacity.
She made me vow solemnly by the saints,
Yea, by all the hierarchy of heaven,
That I would not depart from this your country
Before I had instructed you in the proper cure
For worms, scurvy, rheumatism, heartburn
And other diseases and ailments of the flesh,
That those in England most worthy
In the sight of God, might be advantaged
By her wisdom. I pray you listen.
Take off your caps; give ear,
And gather closer. . . . Note these herbs,
These few poor herbs upon the palm
Of my hand. Nay, sir, do not touch!
I would not have you visited by affliction,
Slain in the instant with your sins

Unshriven! For these herbs,
Scarcely larger than a grain of sand,
Contain such power, such wonder-working
Power—though, I assure you,
With the full cognisance of the Blessèd Mary—
There is no ox of yours, no horse—
Nay, not the stoutest charger in the world—
But if you placed one such upon his tongue
Would die as surely as by the butcher's knife
In lingering agony, so potent are they.
Come, be not afraid. I tell you:
If you follow my instructions to the letter—
To the letter, mark you, and waver not—
No harm shall come to you. Indeed,
I promise you such access of health,
Such manifestations of eternal youth,
That you will bless the day you hearkened
To my instructions. . . . Mark you well.
Leave these for three days only
To steep in good white wine.
If you possess no white, then red,
If not red, then clear spring water—
For I have noted that many a man
Who has no cask of wine in his cellar
Doth own a runnel of water by his door.
After three days, I say, remove them,
Bury them where no child or dog,
Nor any creature you cherish may find them,
And preserve the liquid in an earthen vessel.
Drink from it slowly for thirteen mornings—
Thirteen, mark you—and by the fourteenth
Your varied maladies will disappear,
And what is more—like to myself,
My friends—never return again.

Princess

FIFTEENTH CENTURY

FABULOUS tales they told of her beauty—
  Tales to be spoken by the men of Athens,
Halving the fame of Helen.
Such beauty, they said, the world had not seen,
Not since Guinevere in the courts of Camelot,
Or one word uttered by the Queen of Elfland
Drew men from English lanes.
But she, so beautiful, was dead.
They laid her, still young, small-breasted
And golden-haired, under stones in the chancel
Five centuries ago. They wept,
And the weepers passed, and the weepers' children
Till all was legend, a misted tale
Spun by the troubadour or ballad-singer
With gods and unicorns.

Then, tonight, her tomb was broken:
Lanterns wavering in the darkened Cathedral,
Eight men round an open grave.
For one instant time revolved—
Tintagel and all the towers of Troy!
For there, in her wonder, lay the Princess
Miraculous in beauty, her face
A girl's in golden hair, so beautiful
The heart halted; and for that instant
A wind from heaven.
Then time returned; and as we watched,
Like a vision before our eyes her beauty
Vanished, face fell to dust,
Grey dust. . . . Only
Eight standing at an empty grave,
And a new legend for the tales of men.

Lady Chapel

FIFTEENTH CENTURY

Toward thy chapel,
  Mother of God,
Ever for comfort
  My feet have trod.
      Maid and Mother, attend me there.

Before thine altar
  With candles tall,
I let my cares
  Like a cloak down-fall.
      Maid and Mother, my heart prepare.

I give thee worship,
  Mother and Maid;
On thy compassion
  My sins are laid.
      Maid and Mother, heed my prayer.

Maid, I have loved thee
  Since I was maiden.
Now that with child
  My womb is laden,
      Mother of Christ, thy daughter spare.

Though all unworthy,
  Maiden Mother,
Thy spirit come
  To protect another,
      That I, like thee, a son may bear.

O grant this gift
  That hath no price,
Mary, Queen
  Of Paradise,
      Mother of Heaven, maid most fair!
      Thy servant kneels at the altar stair.

John the Cellarer

FIFTEENTH CENTURY

He's a mean one, our Bishop, though it's not
My place to be saying so, God help me.
Two I've seen throned before, and they feasted us like Princes—
Nothing too good for us, and more than we could hold:
Calves, cranes and capons, pigeons and plovers,
Quail, roebuck, partridges—everything you could wish—
Till we felt like so many Jonahs who had swallowed their whales!
After three days, more dead than alive—but Jesu,
What a death, what a glorious death!
Who wouldn't die in defence of a venison pasty,
Or be martyred on a peacock's wishbone?

          But this man
(God preserve him) why, the victuals he didn't
Order would fill our kitchens for a month. Think of it:
Only a hundred barrels of ale between us,
Where the last man ordered (God rest his soul)
A full three hundred. Five hundred geese
To his two thousand. Ducks, nine hundred
Against three thousand—and so on, all down the list.
Yes, and to make it worse, he's ordered everything
Through the Almoner's office, never a word to me.
Our late Bishop (may he be numbered among the saints)
Talked to me himself. 'Brother John,' he says,
Coming close and shouting. 'This enthronement
Is likely to be my last'—'Oh, no, your Grace,' says I,
Bawling for company, 'Heaven preserve you for Durham.'
'Too late,' he says, giving his head a shake,
'Too old now—too deaf!
Well, this last must be a good one, understand?'
—'Ay, your Grace'—'Plenty to eat and drink,
No stinting, no cheese-paring.'
—'I know, your Grace,' giving him a respectful nudge,

'We'll just make do with the best of everything.'
—'Eh? What's that?'—I hollered into his hairy ear:
'Just make do with the best of everything!'
He laughed fit to kill himself, and finished coughing,
Till I thought he might be taken with a stroke or something
Before he gave his orders.—'Sit down, your Grace.
This chair will hold you. . . . Ah, that's better.
Now get your wind back and tell us what you'd like.'

Lord and Lady

FIFTEENTH CENTURY

TEN thousand years alone,
  He and I,
In our alabaster beds
As the dormant fossils lie.

Round us in the darkness sleeping,
Stone-endued,
Squires and kirtled ladies shared
Our crowded solitude.

Mitred bishops stretched in peace,
Palms together;
Manor-lords lay uncomplaining
Of the heavy limestone weather.

Nobles waisted like their greyhounds,
Grave and tall;
Knights with curving thumb to hilt
Alert for trumpet-call—

All within the hard lake lying,
Without stir,
Waited for Creation's hour
Under Derbyshire. . . .

Then our Genesis began.
One by one
Man's exploring chisel freed
Our bodies to the sun,

Carved the entangling stone away
From lace and fur,
From every flowing fold and line,
To reveal us as we were;

Found the smooth transparency
That nature planned;
Married us in chapel here,
And laid us hand to hand.

The Doom Painting

FIFTEENTH CENTURY

ABOVE the chancel arch
Rise roofs and palaces
Of the heavenly Jerusalem, with a rainbow
Spanning from tower to tower.
On it, aloof (a keystone
To the rainbow's Norman arch)
Sits Christ in glory: holy,
Magnificent, angel-attended,
Judging the quick and dead.
To the right, below him, watching,
The twelve apostles; and under them

79

A graveyard garden, where the righteous
Rise up like tulips from their tombs.
To the left, sinwards, the damned.
They, too, would rise,
But hordes of pitchforked demons
Thrust them, naked, back,
Or drag them, screaming and lamenting,
To a flaming cauldron: miser
Clutching his money-bags,
Ale-wife with short measure,
Cornering merchant—all
Prodded and tossed like cornsheaves
Into the devouring flames. . . .
A clear lesson to us all
Craning and gaping upwards
That even the patience of God
Is exhaustible, and repentance not merely
Virtuous but a sound investment,
Especially in middle age.

The Wool Window

LATE FIFTEENTH CENTURY

ROUND this window you'll search in vain
For a sculptured Adam or painted Cain,
But carved on the stonework and carved there plain
Are carthorse, packhorse, mules and asses,
Bale and woolpack, anchor and chain;
With galleys, galleons, galleasses
Up over the lintel and down again.

Hereabouts in King Henry's reign
I stapled wool from Dorbury Plain
For Flemish loom and Italian skein,

By carthorse, packhorse, mules and asses,
To Britanny, Gascony, Aquitaine,
Or on galleys, galleons, galleasses
Round the coast of France to the ports of Spain.

Boy I came here, in farmer's wain,
A trade to learn and a fortune to gain.
I won them both, so I can't complain
Of the carthorses, packhorses, mules and asses
That served as my troops in the wool campaign,
Nor the galleys, galleons, galleasses
That pulled for my venture and held the strain;

Nor the black-faced sheep who cropped the Plain
In spring and summer, in sun and rain,
To weave me a gown with scarlet train,
So that townsfolk here with their lads and lasses
Would lean from their windows and shout and crane
As I rode to the banquets or Guild Masses
On my horse of grey with the silver rein.

Sailors were drowned and packmen slain,
Beasts by the score have died in pain
For the golden fleeces my barns contain.
Carthorses, packhorses, mules and asses
Built my fine house in Duckpenny Lane;
Galleys, galleons, galleasses
Made me twice Mayor and Mayor again.

*   *   *

Four hundred years my bones have lain
With wife Susannah and daughter Jane,
But over our tomb there still remain
The carthorses, packhorses, mules and asses
To tell of those journeys to France and Spain,
And the galleys, galleons, galleasses
Up over the lintel and down again.

Rood-Loft

IN organ loft
  Both loud and soft
We sing and play,
On Sunday and holiday,
Tunefully, happily
Praising in song
With joy day-long,
Till the Choir doth ring
Like birds in Spring
To our sweet singing.

To wood and string
Our words chiming,
We stand in the middle:
Gittern and fiddle,
Viol and lute,
Citole and flute,
And little bells dangling
With such gay jangling—
All these and psaltery
Strive for sweet mastery.

When that music dies,
Then do arise
In worship and wonder
From chancel under,
Mellow yet strong
In chant and plainsong,
Voices whose notes
Like doves from their cotes
Reach roof and rafter
And Heaven after.

The organ swelling,
God's glory telling,
Next in full voice
Doth cry 'Rejoice.'
Then to this blending
Our own pipes lending,
Anthem we set
And gay motet,
Till all God's ways
Ring loud with his praise.

Strings of the dulcimer
Like threads of gossamer
Tremble most bright
In twilight and candlelight.
Hands of the blowers,
Working like mowers,
Like threshers in valley
Or slaves in a galley,
Move ever faster
For music their master.

Then all together
Our strength we gather
In rood-loft and choir;
And louder, higher,
In sweet accord,
We send to the Lord
From string and wood-note,
From pipe and from throat
Of men and boys,
One joyful noise!

The Wavering Canon

SIXTEENTH CENTURY

THIS man is a feather
   To each wind and weather,
Not for two days together
   Holds to one course.
No wish hath he to search
For living out of church.
He would sooner walk with a lurch
   Than take to his horse.

When the wind is in the east
Then is he a stout priest,
Keeps fast-day and feast
   As well as any Pope.
He does not fail or falter
With Latin from book and psalter,
And for Mass at the altar
   Weareth a rich cope.

But when it veers to the west,
The King's road is best:
Abbeys must be suppressed,
   Their deeds a foul scandal.
Let shrines all be broken,
Their plate seized in token,
And good English spoken
   With no cross or candle.

When it blows from the north,
Then the Roman strides forth;
Our tongue is nothing worth
   In religion and learning.

Those who the Bible read
And question the true creed,
Let no man them heed:
   They are faggots for burning.

Monks and their holy band
Are welcome on every hand;
Restore their house and land,
   Creed, cross and shrine.
Though lechery be rife,
Let a priest take no wife,
But stay chaste all his life
   Except for concubine.

But the wind in the south,
Words change in his mouth.
He upholds the Queen's truth
   Now Pope's truth has gone.
Spent is his priestly vow,
He will not kneel or bow;
Vicar of Christ is now
   Harlot of Babylon.

Thus, Queen or King,
Without great suffering,
With neither hanging nor quartering
   He keeps a fair skin.
From Choir is he not driven,
He stays quick and shriven,
And shall go whole to Heaven
   His crown there to win.

The Queen

Six drums, six trumpets,
   Fanfare for the Queen of England!
A guard of twenty, with gilt axes,
Stand aside at the West entry
And wait, their arms uplifted.
Then come the gentlemen of the Court,
Earls, barons, knights of the garter,
Richly attired and bare-headed.
Next the Chancellor: on one side
An attendant bearing the royal sceptre;
On the other, the sword of state in a red
Scabbard studded with *fleurs de lis*.
Then with a great rustling of the congregation
The Queen enters, her ladies behind her,
Clothed in a gown of white silk
Bordered with pearls as large as mulberries;
And over it a mantle of black silk
Shot with silverthreads. Her train is long
And borne by a Marchioness. For a chain
She wears a collar of gold and jewels,
And on her hair, which is chestnut-coloured,
A small crown of exceeding splendour.

So she walks, and as she passes
The people, like corn, are swathed before her.

The Martins' Chapel

LATE SIXTEENTH CENTURY

THE Martins now are gone,
Their long flight ended.
Into this nest of stone
The last is now descended.

All seasons through
They clung to their one dwelling,
War, peace and plague,
For years past hope of telling.

Now to a land they go
Beyond the farthest swallow.
God grant thy soul a wing
If thou shouldst wish to follow.

Nicholas Martin

LATE SIXTEENTH CENTURY

GOODNIGHT, Nicholas:
Thy day is done.
Under his hill
Goes the westering sun;

Flapping and calling,
The rooks fly home;
Doves in the dovecots
Cry, 'Come, come.'

The taper smokes,
The guests are gone;
Darkness lies
Where the candles shone.

Goodnight, Nicholas:
Long thy sleep.
God in his mercy
Thy slumbers keep.

Bell Tower

i: Morning Bell

POOLS of grey
Where the mead-mists lay
Have drained away;

Winds play
With each scented spray
Of hedgerow may.

No longer stay,
Nor seek to delay
The lift of day,

But when I with gay
Insistence say:
Come pray! pray!
Come pray! . . .
Then rise and obey!

ii: Fire Bell

When in haste you hear me call,
Leave your work, good people all.
Leave the baby in the cradle,
Leave the roast beef on the table,

Leave the cider, leave the cheese,
Leave the crows among the peas.
Down all work at sound of bell:
Find the fire and douse it well.

iii: 'Great Peter'

Peter the Fisher *cast* his net,
His boat did *pitch* when by storms beset.
His judgment *sound* to God he brought,
And on that *rock* our Church was wrought.
Though thrice, in fear, his *tongue* did fail,
For Christ was he tried and *clapped* in jail,
And through the world his gospel *rang*
Till he, at last, on cross did *hang*.
While Death of each man takes his *toll*,
He holds the *keys* of every soul;
So *note* thy words and deeds alike,
And stand by his side when Death doth *strike*.
I, in my tower, his praise shall shout
Till my sound, too, shall peter out.

iv: Storm Bell

When, on a sudden, the day darkens
And thunder threatens the slender spire,
When, high over the sweep of plainland,
Sky is a tangle of forked fire,
When winds rise, and rains hurtle,
And thrush is nested to keep him warm—
Then am I launched on the waves of heaven
To thwart the thunder and quell the storm.

Ironside

MID SEVENTEENTH CENTURY

Bending my head down even to my horse's neck,
  I rode through the West door into the midst of the Church;
Where he, stumbling, striking his hooves upon the pavers
And gravestones therein, it rang like a hollow Forge,
And sent the echoes leaping into the roof thereof.
Thus afrighted, he gave the neigh of a fat priest
At sermon-time, and did drop his dung upon the ground;
Which all the Soldiers seeing did mock at us.
Then they, with siege-ladders and grappling irons
Climbing a window in the South aisle, with their swords
Struck mightily at its lewd images of saints
Which men wantonly had fashioned of painted glass,
And so let God's light into dark places.
As the pieces fell, my horse did plunge again,
And would have thrown me, had I not held him fast
And spoke him words of comfort. Then other soldiers
Seeing this example of their fellows, took their swords
And other like weapons, and smote these blasphemies
Until each Papish window in the South wall
Was but a mass of splinters and tangled lead,
Acceptable unto God. We moved that evening,
Else had we cleansed them all. For even in the transept
A trumpet sounded, summoning to the Market Square.
I was level then with the rood-screen; with a cry
I drew my sword, and setting spur to horse,
Drove for the West door down the stone avenue,
And with a back-stroke served at Marston Moor
Sliced off one nose from that dormitory of bishops,
Drew rein at the last column, and crouching,
Rode into the sun to all men's cheering.
And so it ended. Ay, but that steeplehouse
The hand of the Almighty shall surely pluck down,
And leave not one stone standing upon another.

Wall Monument

SEVENTEENTH CENTURY

THE DAUGHTERS:

Meekly, in descending line,
We kneel behind our mother:
*Agnes, *Rachel, *Susan, *Ann,
One behind the other.

> Stone hood, stone gown,
> Palms met in prayer:
> We, embossed on chancel wall,
> Kneel and worship there.

THE SONS:

Humbly, at our father's back,
We kneel and face our mother;
*William, *Thomas, *Richard, *John,
One behind the other.

> Stone hose, stone gown,
> Palms met in prayer—
> We, embossed on chancel wall,
> Kneel and worship there.

ALL:

Mother, daughters; father, sons;
Pious, meek and dumb,
There we kneel in Sunday peace
Till Domesday come.

* Different voices.

The Pulpit

LATE SEVENTEENTH CENTURY

For Bishop Glynn,
  'The gadfly prelate',
Two parts dandy,
One part zealot,
Decking his creed
With lace and ribbons,
This pulpit was carved
By Grinling Gibbons.
The artist's favourite
Clustered shapes
Of rounded, living,
Luscious grapes
Made many a bored
And drowsy sinner
Long for his port
After Sunday dinner.
But once the Bishop
Had climbed these stairs,
Hopes could not save them
Or fervent prayers.
He had them caught
While he aired his views,
Trapped like lobsters
In rented pews.
He'd gaze with contempt
On their upturned faces,
Straighten his wig
And flounce his laces,
Glare at a cougher,
Pause, and next
Clear his throat
And quote his text.

With tags of Hebrew,
Greek and Latin
He kept them pinned
To the pews they sat in.
Nothing in Testaments
Old or New
But served his purpose
And saw him through—
Epistles, parables,
Gospels, psalms,
He welcomed them all
With open arms.
Every curious
Contradiction,
Snatches of truth
And chunks of fiction,
Appeals to forgive
And commands to kill,
All was grist
To his Sunday mill.

He knew each Jew
And near relation
From Genesis
Until Revelation—
All the rites
And barbarous fights
Of the Israelites
And Ishmelites,
Bedlamites
And Wykhamites,
Stalagmites
And Stalactites—
Every word
That was in the Bible,
Whether divine
Or merely tribal,

Shouts of triumph,
Wails of despair,
Who begot whom
And precisely where—
A mind and memory
Great as his is
Could scoop the jackpot
In all the quizzes.

At notes and footnotes
None was better.
He might miss the spirit,
But never the letter.
He *knew* what it meant
To be a Christian;
Whether he *felt* it's
Another question.
Of Christian love
He had no inkling:
As soon as he spoke
There were cymbals tinkling.
But he loved his Church
And he loved his King—
There just wasn't time
For everything.
These rules were enough
For loyal needs:
'Obey the Church,
Respect her Creeds.'
And on *that* subject
No modern German
Ever turned out
A more tortuous sermon.
Dissecting all
The Thirty-Nine Articles,
He could preach for hours
On each of the particles.

While he admonished
His hurdled flock,
Chimes went unheard
From the chancel clock.
Half hour, one hour,
Two went by
As they gazed at their shepherd
With glazing eye,
Easing buttock
In anguished pew—
And what he was driving at
No-one knew.

When it was done
(For his Lordship brooked
No Norfolk goose
To be overcooked)
He'd smooth his surplice;
And shaking his cuff—
A sign to the faithful
He'd had enough—
Descend the staircase
With regal tread,
So that all who saw him
Proudly said
No previous owner
Of mitre and crozier
Had been such a credit
To tailor and hosier.
With a final flourish
He stalked to his stall,
Half-waking the Dean
And the Canons and all,
And leaving empty
This clustered vine
To Mr Gibbons'
Express design,

Where trailing tendrils
With leaves entwine—
A pulpit bulging
With wooden wine.

Grave-Digger

MANY's the sleeper
I've tucked away
In his six-foot room
At close of day.

Many's the lonely
Bed I've built,
With stone for pillow
And clay for quilt.

And many's the time
I've thought with a sigh
Of my last room taken,
My last guest, I.

'Restorer'

EIGHTEENTH CENTURY

'If you would see his monument, look around you'

STRANGER, pause here, lest as these aisles you pace,
You bring dishonour to th' illustrious race.
Lo! where you walk some fearless Warrior trod,
Or mitred Bishop wing'd his pray'r to God.

And when they died, by Time or Care oppress'd,
This Temple drew them to her stony breast.

Therefore gaze round, 'neath lofty arches stray,
And scan each nook for Trophies of decay.
Though warlike Son lie coffin'd now with Sire,
Though flesh ecclesiastical expire,
Yet marbl'd tomb, which pious orphans raise,
Shall hold their Fame and all their Virtues praise.

Below the Tow'r—let Homage be your guide—
Stands one such monument to filial pride.
One hand on skull, the other laid on plough,
There stands a man with mild and copious brow.
Three Mourners round his sandal'd feet appear,
While Angels waft him to the Heav'nly sphere.

Stranger, pause long, nor scorn to staunch your eyes,
For 'neath this bier the mighty Thompson lies.
Ere God to Man lent that ingenious brain
All was confusion in His holy fane:
Which Thompson, arm'd with Mathematics, saw,
And with a shout, proclaim'd the rule of Law.

From right to left, and left to right he cast
Those stone effusions of th' unletter'd Past;
And rousing inmates from their long repose,
Replac'd them neatly in recumbent rows.
What though one's shinbones found another's knees?
No room for Sentiment when Art decrees.

Some tombs too high, their finials he refin'd;
For those too low, a pedestal design'd;
Until he fashion'd, like Procrustes old,
Their crude proportions to a common mould.
Those worthless, on the rural poor bestow'd,
Became a trough, or deckt some swain's abode.

Next, to the tablets Thompson turn'd his gaze,
The scatter'd relics of less barb'rous days.
Stern Symmetry obey'd her master's call,
And equidistant plac'd them on the wall.
Brasses he banish'd to th' adjacent aisles,
The chancel pav'd with rich Italian tiles.

So from resplendent floor to fretted vault,
No monument withstood his fierce assault;
But each discordant part he did enrol,
And wedded all in one harmonious whole.
Like th' Almighty, His Creation o'er,
Reason now reign'd where Chaos rul'd before.

The Font

THIRTY generations have stood and listened
  By this flowering stone,
Wondering, pondering, as their child was christened;
Would he atone
For all disasters?—their son,
Now cleansed of sin,
Attain the ambitions they never won,
Would never win?

Child after child, generation on generation
Fails and fails.
Always, it seems, the subtle degradation
Of the world prevails.
Faith drowns: soon perish
The dreams they want;
Till they stand with the hopes their fathers cherish
Beside this font.

Some in stealth, raising the cover,
Have stolen water
To turn the thoughts of apprentice lover
Or merchant's daughter.
But in the end, servant or master,
In silk or cotton,
They have lain under marble and alabaster,
Or in graves forgotten. . . .

Yet we see only the outward scheme.
Within the heart
There runs a parallel but opposing stream,
Ours yet apart,
Which flows from eternity and joins it there.
Who, on that level,
Can guess the final triumph or despair
Of God and Devil?

Who can divine through what
Red Seas they crossed,
Or on what ultimate rainbowed Ararat
Each Ark was tossed?
Stand here in faith who need
Such faith. Be reconciled.
Believe that your human love may lead
The inner child.

The Lectern

Forth from my outstretched wings
Fly the words of God.
They are fiercer than mountain eagles,
Softer than doves.

O birds on the air of morning,
Arise and sing!
Send out your murmurs of love,
Your cries of warning,

That when to the branching vault
Like larks you have risen,
Men hearing the pulse of your wings
May halt and listen.

Tell to each hearkening ear,
In this poised hour,
The truth he already knows,
The word of power

That comes to the door of his life
And turns the key:
Speak for his wordless despair
And ecstasy.

Mate with his hovering heart,
O wings of light:
Startle the quick of his soul
To such delight

That the things he has seen and loved,
The ways he has trod,
Are all transformed, transfigured
With the touch of God.

Then home to your eyrie come—
This printed haven
Paged like a plover's tail,
Backed like a raven.

Here on my outstretched wings
Lie still, my birds;
So fierce, so calm, this brood
Of holy words.

Weathercock

HIGH in the stream
Of clouds I stand,
Twirling my tail
At the winds' command.

When West-wind blows
And the swallows flit,
I turn and roast
Like a fowl on a spit.

East-wind cools me:
His breath so raw
That I long for my barn
With its coop of straw.

When North-wind comes,
I see the snow
In its airborne armies
Earthward go.

I watch his cloak,
While I ruffle and freeze,
Cover the domes
Of the cedar trees.

Then South returns,
With the April rain,
To smooth my feathers
To gold again.

Jackdaws, jeering,
Around me flow.
A cuckoo calls
From the elms below.

So, as the seasons
Cool and burn,
I clutch my steeple
And turn, and turn,

Spinning to East,
To West again,
Sighting five counties
From sea to plain;

Reminding men,
As they watch me here,
How St Peter turned
From the wind of fear.

Strange that I
Should be perched instead
Of St John's great bird
Whose wings of dread

Uphold the book
While his words are read,
Four hundred feet
Beneath me spread.

Topsy-turvy,
He and I:
The Eagle earthbound,
The Cock in the sky!

Sundial

South Wall

'TIME is sunlight and a moving shadow;
  Time is rain on warm stone;
Time a spiral of weaving butterflies,
Or fire-smoke after the leaves have gone.

Men make their god in Time's image,
Raise his shrine in every land,
Order their lives to a clock's ticking,
Live and die at his command.

How swift is life on such a reckoning!
Years pass like a driven cloud:
Only a breath, and generations
Exchange their cot-clothes for a shroud.

Love lies under the clock's ticking:
Be still, and know another God.
One moment freed from Time's dominion
Exceeds a year from his measuring-rod.

Mortals, seek that immortal moment!
Crucified by Time's twelve nails
I cannot hasten as man hastens,
And stillness teaches where truth prevails.

O think of time as the rain falling;
As butterflies; or wisps that climb
In autumn from the cairn of leaves;
Sunlight and a moving shadow. . . . Time.'

The Close

SKY, spire, buttress, grass—
Acres of smooth grass.
Lie here in an elm's shadow,
And watch the summer pass.

Thrushes sing in the Canons' gardens;
And beyond their garden walls,
Far, yet clear as a chorister,
The boy-voiced cuckoo calls.

Scent of blossom and mown grass,
Of gently shaken trees—
All the hundred breaths of summer
Borne on the warm breeze.

Across the West-Front wall of stone—
Sunlit, golden stone—
Butterflies in white are dancing,
And a cuckoo flies alone.

The feel of scaly, pine-cone bark,
Of winds that pass unseen
In little soundless waves of air
Over a lake of green.

Acres, acres of smooth grass;
And between that and the sky,
Buttress, wall, tower, spire,
And the white clouds drifting by.

The West Front

IT is, as you see, a cold stone,
Even when time has worked it, indefinite
In colour—hardly stone at all,
But a dull canvas waiting for its painter.
Stand here with me, and watch
How the hours and seasons, weather and sunlight
Change this chameleon stone. How at dawn
It is one substance, but as day comes
The colour ripens—a warm tint
That seems to grow from the stone's kernel,
Till the whole Cathedral is alive with it,
A skin glowing with the building's health.
Through the day, see it blanch
At the storm's coming, as the rain sweeps
Down from the Plain. Then, as it passes,
How blood flows back to the stone,
Calm now, but shining wet
Where the sun strikes. Or at evening,
When mists rise from the twilight meadows,
It assumes the quality of mist—tenuous,
Without substance, like the first dream
Of its creator; a vision only.
But wait till the mists have cleared again,
And over the cedar's shoulder the moon
Appears, gazing with steady eye
At the West Front wall of saints.
Now is the stone the moon's colour;
It glows with unearthly beauty, as if quarried
In the moon's craters. And the saints,
As slowly, imperceptibly, it moves
Among them, seem to be her priests,
Ministering to the mysteries of the night.

Man and his Cathedral

LIKE his cathedral, man
Is held to earth by thrust
And counter-thrust; mortal; enduring;
Destined to return to dust.

But like the spire at night
When Venus comes and Mars,
The fingers of his mind reach up
And pluck the stars.

Prayer

WE pray thee, Spirit of God, that our spirits,
Rising like these arches toward heaven,
May meet in thee, and find stability.
Grant us, through windows of imagination, a glimpse
Of that spaceless, timeless country, from which we came,
To which we shall return. Buttress our belief,
Within this world of time, in that world's values:
Let us feel, within the play of stresses,
That beauty, goodness, truth survive destruction
Of earthly counterparts, and in thy kingdom
Will stand eternally. Open our doors,
O spirit of love, to thy spirit; make us one
With thy creating hand, spirit of life—
That we may be, and know ourselves to be,
A brick, a stone, within thy vast design.

Notes

IN this poem I have tried to build an English cathedral and to suggest the life it held, particularly in the Middle Ages. Although Salisbury is its core, I have not attempted a portrait of any one cathedral but have included features and incidents from many. The following notes are for those who may be interested in the sources.

THE LAND [12]. Salisbury lies at the junction of five streams and is, as one writer has put it, 'as flat as the palm of a man's hand'.

PEASANT'S DAUGHTER [14]. The style is loosely derived from the Anglo-Saxon, which must still have exerted a strong influence on the folk-poetry, as distinct from the court poetry, of the early thirteenth century.

BISHOP [15]. Based on the *Calendar of Papal Registers* (Papal letters of 1198-1304), printed by the Society of Antiquaries. The Bishop is based on Richard le Poore who for seventeen years was Dean of Old Sarum, while his brother was Bishop. They were great-grandsons of a bishop and also, as the soldiers in the poem declare, 'sons of a bishop's concubine'.

QUARRY-MASTER [18]. The underground 'cave quarries' of Chilmark, from which Salisbury was built, described by Edith Olivier in *Wiltshire*. It was a vault of 13 acres, 90 feet high. Professor Lethaby (*Legacy of the Middle Ages*) defines a medieval cathedral as 'a natural growth from a quarry . . . a function of life and not a whim of fashion'.

DEDICATION [19]. From the records of Salisbury Cathedral. *Portrait of Salisbury* by G. H. Cook, and *Salisbury*, by R. L. P. Jowitt. St Vitalis' Day = April 28.

ARCHITECT [21]. The master-mason was responsible for the overall design as well as for the stonework. Chief sources: *The Architect in History*, M. S. Briggs; *Henry Yevele: the Life of an English Architect*, J. H. Harvey; *Gothic Architecture in England*, Francis Bond; *The English Cathedrals*, Felton and Harvey, and Mr Harvey's extraordinary collection of factual titbits, *English Medieval Architects*.

I have taken the latter's view that the less satisfactory parts of Salisbury's design were due to disagreement between the master-mason, Nicholas of Ely, and the dilettante churchman, Elias de Derham; but the credit given to the architect in this dispute is my own interpretation. So is the suggestion that a spire at Salisbury may have been his original intention.

The description of the dawn ceremony is owed to W. A Lawrie's *History of Freemasonry in Scotland*. G. H. Cook (*English Medieval Parish Church*) adds: 'Very few medieval churches face the true equinoctial east, and the Saint's Day theory, if accepted, would account for the diversities of alignment, due to the varying positions of the sunrise from day to day.' 'Who do men say . . . ?' = the opening lines of First Vespers on the Feast of St Peter and St Paul (June 29).

'As girls in Maytime. . . .' This phrase is taken from a thirteenth-century poem on St Hugh of Lincoln, which describes the polished marble columns of the Cathedral: 'Those slender columns which stand round the great piers, even as a bevy of maidens stand marshalled for a dance.'

BALLAD OF THE BISHOP'S TREES [27]. A legend of Winchester Cathedral. In this poem a story of the thirteenth century is told in the ballad-style of the sixteenth.

STONE-CARVER [30]. For this poem I am largely indebted to Professor Nikolaus Pevsner's beautiful book, *The Leaves of Southwell*. Such journeys were not uncommon. Masons often travelled long distances in the interests of their work. M. S. Briggs (*The Architect in History*) tells of Villard de Honnecourt of Cambrai who visited Rheims in the thirteenth century to make sketches 'on his way to work in Hungary'.

WANDERING SCHOLARS [35]. This poem owes much to Helen Waddell's book of the same title, though any errors are mine. Its style and rhythm were suggested by a translation by Wright and Halliwell. 'Paraclete' = the small chapel, named after The Comforter, to which Abelard retired after his emasculation.

CRUSADER [38]. Based on the life of William Longespée the Second, whose cenotaph is in Salisbury Cathedral. All the incidents, including his mother's vision of his death, are founded on fact. *Flos comitum*: 'Flower of Earls', the motto on his tomb. It was a standing joke on the Continent that the English were tailed. 'It seems to have arisen from the legend that St Augustine punished the men of Dorset, who attacked him, by condemning them to have tails.' A. L. Poole, *From Domesday Book to Magna Carta*.

WOOD-CARVER [43]. 'Misericord' (sometimes miscalled 'miserere') = pity or compassion. It was a bracket on the underside of a choir seat which, when tilted up, allowed the occupant to lean against it, standing. Francis Bond (*Wood Carvings in English Churches*, Vol. 1) calculates that in a medieval cathedral or monastery there were '42 periods at which it was necessary to stand daily, besides endless verses and responses, in addition to Matins and Mass'. These misericords represented the spirit's concession to the flesh. Some of the best examples are in Wells, Exeter and

Ely. Those in the poem are quite imaginary: nor is it likely that they would have been carved on the site as described.

CORPUS CHRISTI PLAY [46]. Plays were often performed on Corpus Christi Day (June 4), at first in the church itself, later in the precincts, and finally in the towns. These words are stage directions of the play *Adam*, following very closely the translation of E. K. Chambers in *The Medieval Stage*. They are probably the earliest stage directions in English drama. They also include the following Hamlet-like instructions to the players: 'All the personages must be trained to speak composedly, and to fit convenient gesture to the matter of their speech. Nor must they foist-in a syllable, or clip one of the verses, but must enounce firmly and repeat what is set down for them in due order.'

MARTYR [47]. Imaginary, though Becket may have been the instigator.

SPIRE-BUILDER [48]. Based on the spire at Salisbury, built by Richard Farleigh, 1330. This is a very good illustration of Francis Bond's remark (*Gothic Architecture in England*) that 'the chief problem of medieval builders was not how to erect a building but how to keep it up'. The miracle of Salisbury spire (apart from the original miracle of its beauty) is how it has survived for 600 years. *Portrait of Salisbury*, G. H. Cook; 'The Spire of Salisbury', Geoffrey Grigson, *Country Life*, July 28, 1955. The idea that Farleigh was carrying out the original design of the Cathedral's architect a century before is my invention, and without factual foundation.

THE PEOPLE [51]. A considerable debt to *English Life in the Middle Ages* by L. F. Salzman. 'Yes . . . new hair-style': an almost word-for-word transcription of a sermon by Berthold of Ratisbon, one of the most famous of medieval preachers.

VESPERS [54]. Suggested by a paragraph about Bury St Edmund's in *The Last Abbot*, by A. F. Webling, though the angel comes from another East Anglian church. 'Storm Bell': some bells, blessed by a bishop, had the power of driving off devils and thunderstorms. *Ave, rex*. . . . Vespers began with this antiphon. 'The end of Night': the word is used here symbolically.

PILGRIM [56]. The style of this poem derives, of course, from *The Canterbury Tales*. For its background I am indebted to *Chaucer of England* by Marcuette Chute, and *The Canterbury Pilgrims* by H. S. Ward. Pilgrimages were popular throughout the Middle Ages, not only to Canterbury, but to Walsingham, Compostella, Rome, Jerusalem, and other lesser shrines.

TRAVELLING PREACHER [58]. The first section is based on a statute of Richard II. The rest is the gist of many such sermons, recorded in Froissart's Chronicles and the Chronicon Angliæ, and quoted in Jusserand's *English Wayfaring Life in the Middle Ages*. The couplet is the famous one of John Ball, which played a considerable part in the Peasants' Rebellion.

THE DEVIL [60]. Suggested by an extract from the Chronicle of John of Worcester, 1138, the last line coming direct from G. G. Coulton's translation (*Life in the Middle Ages*).

SANCTUARY [61]. Acknowledgements for the legal facts: *Encyclopædia Britannica*; and *Scenes and Characters from the Middle Ages*, by E. L. Cutts.

CANDLE CAROL [66]. The memory of a realistic crib seen years ago in a church at Woodford Green, Essex. Salisbury

Cathedral once claimed to possess the 'actual' crib from Bethlehem.

PLAGUE-PIT [67]. 'Doctors are now agreed that this was the bubonic plague, coming from the East, and carried by fleas and rats, of which there was no lack in medieval Europe. Medieval medicine was naturally powerless to diagnose anything so dependent upon steady and microscopic observation; the plague was therefore often attributed secondarily to planetary influences and primarily to God's anger against the special wickedness of the age.' G. G. Coulton, *Medieval Panorama*. In this poem I may have melodramatized the speed of death, but have toned down the symptoms of the disease, and have certainly not exaggerated its effects. It is estimated that the outbreak of 1348 left only two million out of a population of five million. Records at Wells Cathedral, where the Bishop remained, tell of 288 parish priests ordained in a single year. As one incumbent died, the Bishop instituted another. *Wells, Glastonbury and Cleeve*, Edward Foord.

RELIQUARY [69]. All the 'relincs' in the poem have been noted by Erasmus (1513) and other travellers in England, not always with approval. Several shrines and reliquaries had the foot-holes mentioned; one still survives at Whitchurch Canonicorum in Dorset. J. A. MacCulloch comments in *Medieval Faith and Fable*: 'The crown of thorns, spear, sponge and reed, the seamless coat, the pillar to which our Lord was bound, the stone of the sepulchre, earth from the Holy Land, even our Lord's footprints, were known from the fourth century. . . . Other relics were Moses' rod and horns, hairs of Noah's beard, pieces of the Ark, soot from the furnace of the Three Children, manna, Job's dung-heap, feathers from St Michael's wings, St Joseph's breath. . . . Christ's tooth, fallen from Him at the age of nine, was at the monastery of Saint-Medard, Soissons.' Boccaccio goes even better and refers satirically to a feather that dropped from Gabriel's wings at the Annunciation and 'a finger of the Holy Ghost'.

THE CLOCK [71]. Two impressions of clocks merge here—one at Wells Cathedral, the other above the Rathaus in Munich before the war. My memory tells me that the figures of jousting knights in the latter were almost life-size. 'Hauberk' = mail tunic of interlocking rings.

CURE-SELLER [73]. Based on an incident quoted in *English Wayfaring Life in the Middle Ages*, by J. Jusserand, translated by L. Toulmin Smith. See also *Medieval Man*, by Frederick Harrison. Salerno was a centre of medical learning in the Middle Ages.

PRINCESS [75]. Imaginary, but the phenomenon has been noted by more than one writer; probably due to a completely airtight sealing of the tomb.

LADY CHAPEL [76]. A large chapel added to the cathedral in honour of the Virgin.

JOHN THE CELLARER [77]. The quantities mentioned are not exaggerated. A menu, quoted in *Medieval Man* by Frederick Harrison, for the enthronement of a bishop includes such items as 4,000 pigeon, 4,000 woodcock, 1,500 pasties, 5,000 dishes of jelly, 6,000 custards, 300 quartens of wheat. The feast would last for days and would probably cost the Bishop the whole of his first year's income. See also *More Medieval Byways*, by L. F. Salzman. At the same time, the priests must not be accused of excessive gluttony. Jocelin of Brakelond records that after the installation of Abbot Samson in Bury St Edmunds in the twelfth century, 'he retired to his chamber, spending his day of festival with more than a thousand dinner guests with great rejoicing'. Quoted in *A History of Everyday Things in England, 1066-1499*, by M. and C. Quennell.

LORD AND LADY [78]. I owe this idea to the following paragraph in Jacquetta Hawkes' great book, *A Land*, and to Henry Moore's illustration which accompanies it:

> The beds of Keuper alabaster are so narrowly limited that I seem to see it throughout geological time with the prelates in their copes and mitres, the wasp-waisted noblemen and knights with lions at their feet, the kilted ladies with their little dogs, together with the forms of Christian iconography, already lying within; negative fossils, shapes waiting for creation instead of surviving from it.

Alabaster was discovered as a material for tomb monuments in the fourteenth century when it began to displace Purbeck marble. Quarried in Derbyshire and Nottingham, it was easy to carve and yet almost indestructible. Its translucency gave it a strangely living quality in changing lights, and its surface lent itself to many varying treatments of tooling and colouring. *English Church Monuments, 1510-1850*, K. A. Esdaile. Where husband and wife are represented, they sometimes lie side by side, the left hand of one turned to touch the right hand of the other.

THE DOOM PAINTING [79]. Most large churches had one in the Middle Ages, usually above the chancel arch. In a period when few could read, these 'visual aids' were an important part of religious education. The one described here still exists in St Thomas's Church, Salisbury. 'Cornering merchant': making a corner in goods at the expense of the community was not considered such a worthy object in those days as it is today and earned the pillory more often than a knighthood.

THE WOOL WINDOW [80]. Suggested by the south porch of Tiverton Church, Devon, and the chapel window in memory of John Greneway, wool merchant, who died in 1529. The external wall has carvings of galleys (rowing boats), galleons (sailing vessels), and galleasses (for both oar and sail), as well as woolpacks and other emblems of his trade. There are excellent photographs in *The West Country*, by Ruth Manning-Sanders.

ROOD-LOFT [82]. The gallery behind the rood or crucifix, containing a small organ, musicians and singers. The chants would usually be supplied, unaccompanied, by the vicars-choral in the choir below. Citole = pear-shaped instrument with four wire strings and ribs. Psaltery = a triangular instrument with ten strings. Motet = in those days an anthem. *Music in the Middle Ages*, by Gustave Reese, and Bond's *Wood Carvings in English Churches*, Vol. 2.

THE WAVERING CANON [84]. The relatively short period from the last years of Henry VIII, through the reigns of Edward VI and Mary to the accession of Elizabeth, was a difficult one for those clergy with no taste for martyrdom. A few on both sides suffered death, imprisonment or exile, but the vast majority played Vicar of Bray until religion settled on a more even keel: *A Short History of English Reformation*, Gordon Crosse; *England in the Age of Wyclife*, G. M. Trevelyan; *Pre-Reformation England*, Maynard Smith. 'Harlot of Babylon' was a term used by extreme Protestants to describe the Pope. The verse-form is one popular at that time.

THE QUEEN [86]. Based on a description by Paul Hentzner, a German visitor to London in 1598, quoted in *Shakespeare's England*, edited by W. Raleigh. The drum and trumpets are from an account of Queen Elizabeth by Sir Robert Sydney, 1600.

THE MARTINS' CHAPEL [87]. The Martin Family, on which this is based, lived at Athelhampton Hall in Dorset for nearly 400 years until the end of the sixteenth century. They are buried in Puddletown Church. I have assumed here that their arms included the usual heraldic birds, martins; in actual fact, this family chose martens, or small monkeys.

NICHOLAS MARTIN [87]. Also suggested by the Puddle-town inscriptions. Nicholas, the last male of the family, died in 1595 and was buried with a two-word epitaph: 'Goodnight, Nicholas'. *Highways and Byways in Dorset,* Sir Frederick Treeves.

BELL TOWER [88]. This was sometimes separate from the Church, as originally at Salisbury. At East Dereham in Norfolk it is actually larger than the church tower. 'Great Peter': there is a bell of this name in Exeter Cathedral which weighs nearly 6 tons, only slightly less heavy than Great Tom at Oxford. The style of this rhyme was not unusual in bell-rhymes. In those days people had no snobbish inhibitions about puns; their appreciation of them was part of their general delight in words. They even italicized them to make sure that no simple person should lose the point.

IRONSIDE [90]. I have tried to weld the vocabulary and prose-rhythm of Nonconformist writers of the seven-teenth century to modern free verse.

WALL MONUMENT [91]. To be seen in many parish churches as well as in cathedrals—the Victorian 'family portrait' two centuries before its time. Here, however, father and mother are seen in profile. They kneel, facing each other, while their sons and daughters arrange them-selves carefully behind in order of seniority.

THE PULPIT [92]. Bishop Glynn is an imaginary person, but his type was extremely common in the late seventeenth and early eighteenth centuries, when the Church was accepted as a safe and fashionable profession, and religion a polite subject for discussion. I had no particular pulpit in mind, but remembered the exquisite carvings that Grinling Gibbons and his pupils left in some City of London churches which I knew before the war. 'There is no instance,' said Horace Walpole, 'of a man before Gibbons who gave the wood the loose and airy lightness of flowers.' But grapes were his favourite models.

RESTORER [96]. A more appropriate epitaph might be: 'May the earth rest heavily upon him.' The prototype of Thompson is, of course, the infamous James Wyatt, called by Pugin 'this monster of architectural depravity'. He has been white-washed in recent years but undoubtedly despoiled many buildings during the eighteenth century with the highest of motives and the complete approval of the Church. The tomb described is imaginary but is also typical of the incongruity of the period.

THE FONT [98]. From the baptismal service of the Church of England: 'Almighty and everlasting God, who of thy great mercy didst save Noah and his family in the ark from perishing by water; and also didst safely lead the children of Israel thy people through the Red Sea, figuring thereby thy Holy Baptism; and by the Baptism of thy well-beloved Son Jesus Christ; in the river Jordan, didst sanctify water to the mystical washing away of sin; We beseech thee, for thine infinite mercies, that thou wilt mercifully look upon this child, wash him and sanctify him with the Holy Ghost, that he, being delivered from thy wrath may be received into the ark of Christ's Church; and being stedfast in faith, joyful through hope, and rooted in charity, may so pass the waves of this troublesome world, that finally he may come to the land of everlasting life, there to reign with thee world without end.' Because the baptismal water was sometimes stolen for white magic or black, wooden font-covers with locks were added, wood being also a medium difficult for witchcraft to penetrate.

THE LECTERN [99]. Usually carved in the form of an eagle, the symbol of St John.

THE WEST FRONT [105]. I had in mind again the appearance of Salisbury Cathedral at night, though the statues may have moved across from Wells. Edith Olivier, in her *Wiltshire*, writes of the stone at Salisbury: 'It seems hardly a stone at all, but the visible impression of the building constructed from it.'